ELEANOR ROOSEVELT

Eleanor Roosevelt. (Franklin D. Roosevelt Library)

MAKERS OF AMERICA

ELEANOR ROOSEVELT

A Passion to Improve

RAY SPANGENBURG
& DIANE K. MOSER

Facts On File, Inc.

Eleanor Roosevelt: A Passion to Improve

Facts On File, Inc.
11 Penn Plaza
New York NY 10001

Library of Congress Cataloging-in-Publication Data
Spangenburg, Ray
    Eleanor Roosevelt : a passion to improve / Ray Spangenburg and Diane K. Moser.
        p. cm.—(Makers of America)
    Includes bibliographical references (p.   ) and index.
    Summary: Describes the life and significant achievements of the woman who helped transform the role of first lady.
        ISBN 0–8160–3371–4
        1. Roosevelt, Eleanor, 1884–1962—Juvenile literature.
    2. Presidents' spouses—United   States—Biography—Juvenile literature. [1. Roosevelt, Eleanor, 1884–1962. 2. First ladies.]
    I. Moser, Diane, 1944– . II. Title. III. Series.
    E807.1.R48S68 1997
    973.917'092—dc20
    [B] 96–16381

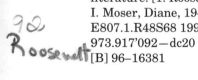

Text design by Catherine Rincon
Cover design by Matt Galemmo

This book is printed on acid-free paper.

Printed in the United States of America

MP FOF 10 9 8 7 6 5 4 3 2 1

*This one for Sherry Roberts,
who knows the wonderful mysteries
of love and life.*

CONTENTS

ACKNOWLEDGMENTS

A book is a team effort and many different hands and minds have helped with this one. Ideas and insights come from everywhere, enthusiasms build energy, and helpful expertise often saves the day. In particular we'd like to thank Karen Burtis and Mark Renovitch at the Franklin D. Roosevelt Library for excellent photo research on a series of bitter cold winter days; Emily Spectre, our project editor at Facts On File, who jumped in with verve to see the book through manuscript and production phases; Faith K. Gabriel, our copy editor, for her pursuit of detail (some of which we may still have overlooked, through no fault of hers); and Bernard Gough, for his encouragement.

PROLOGUE

On March 6, 1933, two days after the first inauguration of Franklin Delano Roosevelt as president of the United States, Eleanor Roosevelt strode into the Red Room at the White House. The room was filled with 35 invited reporters, all women, all curious, some a little annoyed to be participating in a "women only" event. Eleanor Roosevelt passed around a

The first president's wife to hold press conferences, here Eleanor Roosevelt (center) meets with a group of reporters at the White House in 1933. (Franklin D. Roosevelt Library)

box of candies, and so began the first news conference ever held by the wife of a president. So also began Eleanor Roosevelt's long, impassioned battle against the fetters of tradition in Washington, a gently but firmly fought battle to retain her independence and to build her own sphere of influence. This day marked the beginning of a remarkable White House career, in a position that had never before held any significance. During the following 12 years, Eleanor Roosevelt would transform what had once been an entirely passive, peripheral role into an active influence for social change. In her role as activist, she would become both one of the most beloved figures of her time and arguably the most effective First Lady of any time.

Two days earlier, Inauguration Day had dawned cold and bleak, and Eleanor had approached the day with misgivings. Looking back on the moment on election night when victory became clear, she later wrote: "The turmoil in my heart and mind was rather great." The White House, she felt, could become a prison. As a public person having no real role, she would not have the freedom to live as she wanted or go where she wanted. For years, she and Franklin had not had a traditional marriage, operating more like partners than husband and wife, and she had developed a strongly independent style of life. Now she greatly feared losing that independence. Her somber mood contrasted distinctly with the jubilance of those who had elected her husband president of the United States and now waited in hope—hope that a change in government would make their world better, relieve them from the Great Depression, now at its worst.

"I never wanted to be a president's wife, and I don't want it now," she had told Associated Press reporter Lorena Hickok in an interview two days after the election. "For him I am deeply and sincerely glad. I shouldn't have had it go otherwise. And now I shall start to work out my own salvation. . . ."

ELEANOR ROOSEVELT

DARK CHILDHOOD
1884–1899

The 20th century was more than 15 years away when Anna Eleanor Roosevelt was born on October 11, 1884. The Eiffel Tower hadn't been built, and the Wright Brothers had not yet constructed the plane they would fly at Kitty Hawk. People still lit their houses by gaslight and used horse-drawn carriages to make their way around the crowded New York City streets. Women wore floor-length dresses and could not vote.

Eleanor came into the world only 24 years after the end of the Civil War, and if President Abraham Lincoln had survived the bullet wounds inflicted by John Wilkes Booth, he would have celebrated his 75th birthday the year she was born. From Britain, Queen Victoria ruled a vast empire, while in the United States of America, President Chester Alan Arthur resided in the White House. Mark Twain had just published *The Adventures of Huckleberry Finn*. And on Bedloe's Island in New York Harbor, workers were busy laying the foundation for the Statue of Liberty, a gift from the people of France, which would arrive dismantled and packed in over 214 gigantic packing cases during the following year.

The times, however, were changing. Mixed with the steady traffic of horse-drawn vehicles, cable car systems began to spread through city streets, carrying over 400 million passengers annually in 1884, and within 10 years, Henry Ford would manufacture his first automobile. The first skyscraper (consid-

Eleanor's parents, Elliott and Anna Hall Roosevelt, in a posed portrait typical of their time. (Franklin D. Roosevelt Library)

ered "towering" at 10 stories) was nearing completion in Chicago; it would open officially in 1885. And only four years earlier, in 1880, Thomas Alva Edison had installed his exciting new electrical lighting system in an experiment that lit the streets of Wabash, Indiana, and later, a full mile of New York City's Broadway. By 1889, in fact, the first electric lights would be installed in the White House. (President Benjamin Harrison, though, would refuse to touch the switches—too dangerous, he contended; that task was assigned to a hapless employee.)

Eleanor's parents, Anna and Elliott Roosevelt, were members of New York City's elite social circle, "swells" as the less well-to-do called them with a mixture of envy and admiration. It was a time when many people followed the activities of wealthy and socially prominent families with the same fascination reserved today for movie and rock stars. At the time of their marriage, Anna was 19, spoiled and beautiful. Elliott, 23, was charming and known among his friends as a good-natured sportsman and playboy. It was a match well fitted for high society. Both families were wealthy, with long and honorable histories: Anna, a descendant of the Livingstons, a distinguished New York family, and Elliott, the younger brother of Theodore Roosevelt (soon to be president of the United States). "Uncle Teddy" wasn't close to his younger brother, whom he considered "a sissy," but he was named Eleanor's godfather at the time of her birth and always remained particularly fond of her, if not of her father.

Young Eleanor greatly appreciated Uncle Teddy's affection, for despite outward appearances, all was not happy in her parents' marriage. Neither Elliott nor Anna was well suited for parenthood, and despite the birth of two other children, both sons—Elliott, born in 1889, and Gracie Hall (known as Hall), born in 1891—the marriage quickly deteriorated.

Elliott was a loving and affectionate father, with a warm and special attachment to his young daughter, but he was never able or willing to face the responsibilities of family life. Having grown up in the shadow of his outgoing and aggressive older brother, he had been an extremely sensitive child, often subject to the bullying of others, including brother Teddy who was outspokenly uncomfortable with what he saw as his younger brother's too "effeminate" nature. His brother's judgment wasn't softened when Elliott suffered a series of (possibly epileptic) attacks in adolescence, leaving him dependent on drugs and, later, alcohol for comfort and relief. Elliott also sought relief from what he considered the demanding pressures of married life by taking long hunting trips, playing cards and paying frequent visits to New York City's many nightclubs.

By the time Eleanor was seven, shortly after her brother Hall's birth in 1891, Elliott and Anna had separated. The separation, however, did nothing to decrease young Eleanor's adoration of her wandering father. His gentleness and deep, if undependable, love for her would leave an indelible mark on her life. To her, he would always be a very special person, the one that she had always loved the most, and the one person, until the time of her own death, that she had most freely felt love and uncritical affection for. Remembering the days before her parents' separation, Eleanor wrote:

> I was a shy, solemn child even at the age of two, and I am sure that even when I danced I never smiled. My earliest recollections are of being dressed up and allowed to come down to dance for a group of gentlemen who applauded and laughed as I pirouetted before them. Finally, my father would pick me up and hold me high in the air. He dominated my life as long as he lived, and was the love of my life for many years after he died.
>
> With my father I was perfectly happy. . . . We had a country house at Hempstead, Long Island, so that he could hunt and play polo. He loved horses and dogs, and we always had both. . . . He was the center of my world and all around him loved him.

Now with just her mother and two younger brothers, it seemed to Eleanor that much of the warmth of her life had gone with the absence of her father. Although she was deeply fond of her younger brothers, her relationship with her mother was often uncomfortable and strained.

Left alone to raise her family, Anna did her best. What money could buy for the children it bought: expensive clothes, tutoring and vacation trips. But what it couldn't buy was repair for the loss of affection that Eleanor now felt in her life. Although Anna genuinely loved her three children, and tried her best to make up for the loss of their father, she was not able to establish the much-needed bond between herself and her seven-year-old daughter.

A stunningly beautiful and gracious woman, still very young, Eleanor's mother was a product of the late Victorian age, and she held on to many values of her social set that were rapidly becoming outdated. Remembering many years later in her autobiography, Eleanor wrote, not without bitterness, "My mother belonged to that New York City society which thought itself all-important. Old Mr. Peter Marié, who gave choice parties and whose approval stamped young girls and young matrons a success, called my mother a queen, and bowed before her charm and beauty, and to her this was important."

Eleanor, with her increasing shyness, her strong, plain features and tall, gangly body, was a source of discomfort and concern to her attractive, feminine and socially adept young mother. Having inherited her father's sensitivity, Eleanor was quick to pick up on her mother's discomfort and explained her own unhappiness many years later when recalling the "curious barrier" that she felt existed between herself and her mother. As she recalled evenings with her mother sitting in the family parlor with her brothers or visitors, she wrote: " . . . still I can remember standing in the door, very often with my finger in my mouth—which was, of course, forbidden—and I can see the look in her eyes and hear the tone of her voice as she said: 'Come in, Granny.' If a visitor was there she might turn and say: 'She is such a funny child, so old-fashioned, we always call her Granny.' I wanted to sink through the floor in shame . . ."

And then suddenly in 1892, already shaken by the separation from her father, eight-year-old Eleanor experienced another blow. Her mother became ill with diphtheria. Within a few days, at the age of 29, the young and beautiful Anna Hall Roosevelt was dead. Unable to carry the responsibilities of raising the children, Elliott agreed to his wife's last wish and permitted Eleanor and her two brothers to be moved to the home of their maternal grandmother.

It was not a happy decision. If her parents were ill-suited to raising children, Mary Hall—"Granny Hall," as Eleanor called her—was even less so. Living as a virtual recluse in a "gloomy Manhattan brownstone," at 49, Granny Hall was still struggling with the eccentricities and drinking habits of her own two grown sons, both of whom still lived with her for long periods at a time. A severe, old-fashioned woman, if Granny Hall had failed at giving guidance to her own children, she was determined to be all the more strict and spartan with the lives of her new charges.

Life in the brownstone was both gloomy and unhappy, relieved only by the occasional visit from Eleanor's father.

> Though he was so little with us, my father dominated all this period of my life. Subconsciously I must have always been waiting for his visits. They were irregular, and he rarely sent word before he arrived, but never was I in the house, even in my room two long flights of stairs above the entrance door, that I did not hear his voice the minute he entered the front door. Walking downstairs was far too slow. I slid down the banisters and usually catapulted into his arms before his hat was hung up.

For the most part though, the depression in the Hall house was unrelenting. Remembering those days, one of Eleanor's cousins later wrote: "My mother would ask me to go to have supper with Eleanor. . . . I never wanted to go. The grim atmosphere of that house. There was no place to play games, unbroken gloom everywhere. We ate our suppers in silence." A classmate of Eleanor's later described the house as "grim and ill-kept," adding, "nobody cared how it looked."And Eleanor recalled:

> a dark basement, and inadequate servants' quarters with working conditions which no one with any social conscience would tolerate today. The laundry had one little window opening on the backyard, and of course we had no electric light. We were modern in that we had gas! The servants' room lacked ventilation and comfortable furnishings. Their bathroom was in the cellar, so each one had a basin and a tiny pitcher in a tiny bedroom. . . . The dining room, in the extension in the back, was quite a bright room, having three windows on the side. Back of that was the pantry, where I spent considerable time, for the butler, Victor, was kind to me and taught me how to wash dishes and wipe them, though when I broke one he was much displeased.

Eleanor (right) ca. 1892, with her attentive father and brothers, Elliott (left) and baby Hall. (Franklin D. Roosevelt Library)

Eleanor would later write about this period: "Looking back I see that I was always afraid of something; of the dark, of displeasing people, of failure. Anything I accomplished had to be done across a barrier of fear."

Within a year after moving into the Hall house, Eleanor lost another member of her family, her four-year-old brother, Ellie (Elliott). "My little brother Ellie never seemed to thrive after my mother's death. Both he and the baby, Hall, got scarlet fever . . . ," Eleanor recalled. "The baby got well without any complications, but Ellie developed diphtheria and died."

These difficult years were made only occasionally brighter when the Hall family would spend summers at their country house called Tivoli. It was a gigantic, rambling place, situated high on a bluff overlooking the Hudson River north of New York City. Describing it later, Eleanor remembered it as " . . . big, with high ceilings and a good many rooms, most of them large. My grandmother had furnished it downstairs in a rather formal way. There were some lovely marble mantelpieces and chandeliers for candles. We had neither gas nor electricity. We had lamps, but often went to bed by candlelight. . . ." A well-stocked library helped to make the summer days pass pleasantly, and young aunts and uncles brought more fiction for the youngsters. "It is astonishing," Eleanor later recounted, "how much Dickens, Scott and Thackery were read and reread. . . ."

The house was large, with nine bedrooms for the family on the second and third floors in addition to five rooms for servants. "There were just two bathrooms in this large house," Eleanor recalled, "but it never occurred to us that it was an inconvenience or that it really made much work to have to use basins and pitchers in our own rooms."

Even at Tivoli, though, Eleanor remained tightly bound by the stern guidance of Granny Hall, who dictated the lives of the children with a strong and rigid hand. In turn, Granny Hall guided herself by her unflagging belief in the righteousness of long-standing Victorian customs and her dogmatic faith in the Bible. "She really believed every word in the Bible," Eleanor later recounted. "She believed the whale really swallowed Jonah." Still, the bright expanses of Tivoli were a welcome escape from the gloomy confines of Granny Hall's Manhattan brownstone. And so were the letters that Eleanor received, not as frequently as she would have liked, from her father. (Later in her life she would collect those treasured letters and publish them.) And, sometimes, unexpectedly, he would even visit, and, for a brief while, her world would be brighter and full of hope.

Even this happiness, though, was short-lived, with her father disappearing as suddenly as he had come, leaving her to wait for the next visit, the next letter. And sometimes it would be a long time between visits or letters.

The truth was that Elliott Roosevelt was quickly losing control of his life. By now a full-fledged alcoholic, trapped in a downward spiral, he had few places to turn for help. Plagued by despair over his own "weakness," Elliott began moving from town to town and job to job in an increasingly self-destructive plunge. He barely managed to escape forcible confinement to an institution by his unbending and self-righteous brother Teddy. The inevitable end came, as Eleanor remembered it many years later:

> On August 14, 1894, just before I was 10 years old, word came that my father had died. My aunts told me, but I

simply refused to believe it, and while I wept long and went to bed still weeping I finally went to sleep and began the next day living in my dreamworld as usual.

My grandmother decided that we children should not go to the funeral, and so I had no tangible thing to make death real to me. From that time on I knew in my mind that my father was dead, and yet I lived with him more closely, probably, than I had when he was alive.

For the rest of her life she would keep the memory of her father alive, the one bright spot in the unhappiness of her childhood.

2

INTO THE SUNLIGHT
1899–1902

Life at Granny Hall's continued to be rigid, confined and depressingly claustrophobic, relieved only a few times each year when Eleanor was expected to attend the annual picnics, dances or holiday festivities given by other members of the Roosevelt clan. Looking back on those festivities later in her life, Eleanor still remembered the bright spots they provided in her otherwise drab existence. Even those memories, though, contained a touch of sadness as she recalled her awkwardness and discomfort, dressed in drab clothes, "practical" shoes, her dresses usually too short for her tall skinny body, not knowing the latest popular fads or music and set apart even more by her ever-increasing shyness. Later, recalling one of those family gatherings, Eleanor wrote: "I was a poor dancer, and the climax of the party was a dance. What inappropriate dresses I wore—and, worst of all, they were above my knees. I knew, of course, that I was different from all the other girls and if I had not known they were frank in telling me so!" Self-conscious about her appearance, feeling always an outsider among both adults and her contemporaries, young Eleanor often felt that life held no specialness for her, no uniqueness—that she was destined forever to be "Granny," the unwanted child hesitating in the doorway, alone, different and useless.

Mlle. Marie Souvestre, whose photograph Eleanor kept on her bed stand throughout her lifetime. (Franklin D. Roosevelt Library)

And then one day, as Eleanor recalled, "Suddenly life was going to change for me. My grandmother decided that the household had too much gaiety for a girl of fifteen. She remembered that my mother had wanted to send me to Europe for a part of my education. Thus the second period of my life began." In 1899, it wasn't unusual for young girls of Eleanor's social class to be sent to Europe for some of their education. And so the 15-year-old Eleanor found herself on the way to what she would long remember afterward as one of the happiest and most important periods of her life.

In the fall of 1899, Eleanor set out to cross the Atlantic on the first stage of her adventure, an ocean voyage aboard a luxury liner. Assigned to travel with an aunt, who was also on her way to England, the shy and overly protected 15-year-old had no idea what to do or expect. "She took me in her cabin and told me that she was a poor sailor and always went to bed immediately on getting on the boat. I thought this was the proper procedure and followed suit. As a result, I did not enjoy that trip at all, as most of it was spent in my berth, and I arrived in England distinctly wobbly . . ."

Allenswood, the school that had been selected for Eleanor's European education, was a small exclusive girls' school located near Wimbledon Commons on the outskirts of London. Its founder, headmistress and principal educator was a short, stout, impeccably groomed French woman, Marie Souvestre, known simply as Mlle. Souvestre to her students and admirers. In her early seventies at the time of Eleanor's arrival, Mlle. Souvestre was the daughter of Emile Souvestre, a French writer who had been exiled to Switzerland as a result of his antimonarchist views during the 1848 French revolution. Like her father, Marie Souvestre was strong-minded, outspoken and liberal. Gifted with a charismatic and refined personality, along with a commanding demeanor, she would remain legendary in the minds of her students and all who knew her. Left, since the death of her father, without an adult she could admire and feel true affection for, young Eleanor was immediately captivated. ". . . [S]he had snow-white hair. Her head was beautiful, with clear-cut, strong features, a strong face and broad forehead. Her hair grew to a peak in front and waved back in natural waves to a twist at the back of her head. Her eyes looked through you, and she always knew more than she was told."

For her own part, Mlle. Souvestre, who always demonstrated a special affinity for American children, took an instant liking to the gawky teenager. Seeing beyond Eleanor's shyness and self-consciousness, she was quick to perceive the young student's agile mind and her deep reserves of dignity and natural curiosity.

And responding, young Eleanor began to open up. Now far from the rigidity and gloominess of Granny Hall's iron-handed domain, and freed from the spell of past judgments, she began to discover her own true character. She found traits that went deeper than the more superficial aspects of "personality": her sincere feelings for others and strong sense of social justice, her respect for intelligence and honesty and her sensitivity to others who for one reason or other, like her, didn't always fit into easily assigned social roles.

In a short time, too, she had friends, her first real ones, among the school's other students, often finding flowers left, as was the school's custom, in bright bunches in her room. In a few brief months after leaving America, life for Eleanor had changed dramatically. Allenswood was like stepping out of a dark and gloomy house into a brightly lit summer garden.

Here, too, the academic ambiance was both demanding and exciting. One of the school's disciplines was that all the students should speak only in French, and each student was on the honor system to report herself if ever the rule was breached.

Although there were other teachers and classes, Eleanor always looked forward most to those taught by Mlle. Souvestre. Eleanor later recollected:

> Mlle. Souvestre held her history classes in her library, a charming and comfortable room lined with books and filled with flowers, looking out on a wide expanse of lawn, where really beautiful trees gave shade in summer and formed good perches for the rooks and crows in winter.
>
> We sat in little chairs on either side of the fireplace. Mlle. Souvestre carried a long pointer in her hand, and usually a map hung on the wall. She would walk up and down, lecturing to us. We took notes, but were expected to do a good deal of independent reading and research. . . . This was the class we enjoyed beyond any other.

These were important years for Eleanor, and key years, too, for a world that now was quickly changing as the century turned. One of the major events of the early 1900s came for the Roosevelt family when Uncle Teddy, who had been elected vice president of the United States in 1900, became president in September 1901 after the assassination of President William McKinley. Far away in England, though, the event that Eleanor remembered most in 1901 was the funeral of Queen Victoria, which she watched from the home of relatives living in London. Years later she wrote: "I shall never forget the genuine feeling shown by the crowds in the streets or the hush that fell as the gun carriage bearing the smallest coffin I had ever seen came within our range of vision. Hardly anyone had dry eyes as that slow-moving procession passed by, and I have never forgotten the great emotional force that seemed to stir all about us as Queen Victoria, so small of stature and yet so great in devotion to her people, passed out of their lives forever."

A group of Eleanor's classmates, gathered during the summer of 1900 on the grounds of Allenswood, the school she attended in England. (Franklin D. Roosevelt Library)

It was the end of an era in England and the world.

And now nearly 17 years old, Eleanor, too, was changing. The energetic Marie Souvestre decided to visit southern Europe in the spring of 1901, taking Eleanor along as her companion, a plan Eleanor described as "one of the most momentous things that happened in my education." They traveled down to Marseilles, then along the Mediterranean, making stops in Pisa and in Florence, where they stayed with a friend of Mlle. Souvestre's who was an artist living in a villa perched high on a hill overlooking the city.

It was a trip that Eleanor, once a frightened and sheltered child, never forgot. In Marseilles, she and Mlle. Souvestre walked along the quai and soaked up the atmosphere of a great fishing port, with its ships from foreign lands and little fishing boats with brightly colored sails. They saw a little church where local families made offerings for the preservation of their loved ones at sea. They stopped at a small café, where they dined on bouillabaisse, a delicious favorite of the French workers, which Eleanor described as "a kind of soup in which every possible kind of fish that can be found in nearby waters is used."

Mlle. Souvestre knew how to bring out responsibility and independence in her young charge—by giving her real responsibility. As Eleanor later recalled in her autobiography: "She was an old lady and I was sixteen. The packing and unpacking for both of us was up to me, once we were on the road. I looked up trains, got the tickets, made all the detailed arrangements necessary for comfortable traveling." The self-reliance and confidence she gained was a valuable lesson that Eleanor drew on throughout her life.

One of the most memorable moments was the visit to Florence. Pleading fatigue, Mlle. Souvestre insisted that Eleanor could only learn about a city by walking its streets. "Florence is worth it," she told her young companion. " . . . go see it. Later we will discuss what you have seen." And so off Eleanor went, " . . . sixteen years old, keener than I have probably ever been since and more alive to beauty, I sallied forth to see Florence alone."

"Though I was to lose some of my self-confidence and ability to look after myself in the early days of my marriage," she would later recall, "it came back to me later more easily because of these trips with Mlle. Souvestre."

It had been a happy three years for Eleanor, perhaps the happiest of her life, but all too soon they had to come to an end. Word came from Granny Hall that she expected Eleanor to return the summer before her 18th birthday and prepare for her official "coming out," the traditional festivities of Eleanor's social class when young girls turning 18 were "introduced" to society in a series of gala affairs. And although she dreaded the whole idea and had hoped to spend a fourth year with Mlle. Souvestre, it was neither in young Eleanor's nature or social conditioning to argue or refuse. As a Roosevelt she was expected to take her rightful place in the elite social world, to obey its long-standing rules and traditions and to meet her obligations as a young debutante.

Early in the summer of 1902, she reluctantly sailed for home.

3

RETURN AND ROMANCE
1902–1905

The Hall household had changed by the summer of Eleanor's return in 1902. By this time, Granny Hall had almost entirely closed down her Manhattan house and had moved more or less permanently to the summer residence at Tivoli on the Hudson. Granny Hall's two sons, Eleanor's uncles—always a little on the wild side during her years at the Hall house—had turned into full-fledged alcoholics. The change in Uncle Vallie, who had always shown kindness to her in the past, hit her particularly hard. Now he often drank so heavily that he careened far out of control, shooting his guns from the upstairs windows, aiming wildly and drunkenly at anything he saw moving across the lawn.

Eleanor had seen the impact of alcoholism before, but even when drinking, her father had always remained gentle and kind. The exposure now to Vallie and the violent destructiveness of his alcoholic episodes was to have a lasting effect on her life. "This was my first real contact with anyone who had completely lost the power of self-control," Eleanor would recall years later, "and it began to develop in me an almost exaggerated idea of the necessity for keeping all one's desires under complete subjugation."

Despite Granny Hall's failures with her own children, or perhaps because of it, she was as determined as ever to continue her strict control over Eleanor's life. But Eleanor was no longer a young child. At 18, she had reached the age at which, among those in her social circle, she was thought of as a debutante whose formal "coming out" into society was planned for that fall. Everyone, including Granny Hall, expected her now to fit into and flow with the social whirl of high society.

For the most part, coming out meant a nearly unending round of dances, formal dinners, parties and social functions—including presence at openings of the theater, ballet and opera, attendance at accepted benefits and always visiting the "right" people and being visited by them. Now grown to her full height of close to 5 feet 11 inches, with a trim and shapely figure, thick, full hair and expressive eyes, Eleanor was no longer the gawky and awkward "Granny" her mother had made fun of. She had become a striking young woman.

Still shy, Eleanor preferred not to be the center of attention, but she had nevertheless learned to mitigate much of that shyness by warmly encouraging others around her to talk while she quietly and attentively listened. It was an effective maneuver, quickly earning her a reputation among her peers as a "good listener" and a "sympathetic ear," while at the same time allowing her to learn from others. There were some side effects to this self-protecting device, however, both good and bad, as she later recalled:

> More and more, as I grew older, I used the quickness of my mind to pick the minds of other people and use their knowledge as my own. A dinner companion, a casual acquaintance, provided me with information which I could use in conversation, and few people were aware how little I actually knew on a variety of subjects that I talked on with apparent ease.
>
> This is a bad habit, and one which is such a temptation that I hope few children will acquire it. But it does have one great advantage; it gives you a facility in picking up information about a great variety of subjects and adds immeasurably to your interests as you go through life.

Not all of her time was taken up with social activities. In the early 1900s, reform was in the air. Suffragists had begun campaigning for women's right to vote and other reforms in the 1840s and by now had gained some ground, but the nation's population was swelling rapidly and working conditions, especially in the cities, were notoriously poor. By the turn of the century, the population of Greater New York had swelled to 3.5 million. Many were immigrants who had arrived penniless, unable to bargain for better living and working conditions. Fully two-thirds of New York City's population lived crammed into shabby tenement buildings on the Lower East Side in Manhattan, often in windowless, gloomy rooms. The wealthy young women in Eleanor's social group were expected to put in a certain amount of time addressing the problems of those less fortunate than themselves. Most of them met this expectation by becoming active in some of the programs offered by such charity groups as the Junior League, and Eleanor was no exception.

Founded by Mary Harriman in 1900, the Junior League of the New York College Settlement was originally established to aid a local settlement house. Settlement houses were centers set up for charitable work in so-called underprivileged areas. The idea caught on quickly and soon other Junior League branches in Baltimore, Brooklyn, Philadelphia and Boston sprang up. By 1920 there would be 39 Junior Leagues in the United States, all engaged in various civic improvement projects.

While not all the debutantes who joined the league were active in its programs (some merely allowed the use of their prestigious names or contributed money to the league programs), Eleanor joined in actively. Traveling by the elevated railway or by streetcar, she made her way regularly to the settlement house on Rivington Street in New York City where she taught after-school classes for children in calisthenics and sewing. She also joined the league's crusades against oppressive working conditions and child labor. Many workers in private businesses and factories at that time faced a 14-hour work day, six days a week, for a weekly wage of six dollars. The league pressed—successfully in many cases—for a shorter work day of 10 hours and equal pay for equal work. The young women also campaigned for child labor laws that would end the practice of setting children as young as four or five years old to work in appalling conditions, spending long hours for little pay making artificial flowers or similar tasks.

Eleanor's contemporaries saw her as a helpful young woman with dignity, using words like "affectionate," "simple" and "spontaneous" to describe her during this time. She made her way earnestly but haltingly in her Junior League responsibilities—completely unfamiliar as she was with the life of anyone who worked for a living. But she enjoyed the children she taught and glowed at their appreciation of her and her interest in them, and she felt critical of some of her peers who did not relish being with the children as she did.

The social season that began in the autumn of 1902 brought another important element into Eleanor's life—a reacquaintance with her cousin, Franklin Delano Roosevelt. Not close cousins (he was a member of a distant branch of the same family tree), Franklin and Eleanor had not seen each other often as children, but she had first begun to attract his attention when he was 16 and she was 14. At that time, a student at Groton preparatory school, Franklin was already impressed—as he commented to his mother after a family gathering, "Eleanor has a good mind."

By the time Eleanor had returned from Allenswood, Franklin was a junior at Harvard University, and he began to make a point of turning up at the social gatherings in New York that formed part of the coming-out process for his female peers. Eleanor was one of five young Roosevelt women to become debutantes in 1902, so he had ample family excuses for making the trip to New York several times that fall. Eleanor's name began to turn up frequently in his diary, and he made a point of seeing that she was included on the invitation list to gatherings at his family's house.

Franklin Delano Roosevelt was a tall, slender, handsome young man with gray blue eyes and an athletic physique. His mother's family, the Delanos, lived on the Hudson at Newburgh, New York. Their heritage dated back to Warren Delano, a New Bedford sea captain in the early 1800s. Sara Delano Roosevelt's father had made more than a million dollars in trade with China, lost it, and made it again. At her father's death, Sara inherited more than a million dollars. Fully conscious of this and of the prominent position his father's family had enjoyed since Dutch colonial days before the Revolutionary War, Franklin exuded a jaunty self-confidence and patrician air. "Cousin Theodore," whose election to the presidency had occurred during Franklin's Groton years, had caught his imagination and served as an early role model. Now the president's favorite niece also had caught his attention.

Franklin and Eleanor in August 1904, on the porch at Campobello during their courtship days. (Franklin D. Roosevelt Library)

By the fall of 1903, Franklin found more and more excuses to spend time with Eleanor, helping her settle her younger brother, Hall, at Groton, his own alma mater. Franklin invited Eleanor and Hall for the Harvard-Yale game in Cambridge, an invitation she accepted on condition that proper chaperones would also be present. After the game, Eleanor and Hall returned to Groton, but the next day, Sunday, November 22, Franklin followed her down to Groton and spent the day with her. They attended church together in the morning and went to chapel together that evening. Sometime during the course of that day he proposed marriage.

Eleanor would later write about that day:

> I had a great curiosity about life and a desire to participate in every experience that might be the lot of a woman. There seemed to me to be a necessity for hurry; without rhyme or reason I felt the urge to be a part of the stream of life, and so in the autumn of 1903, when Franklin Roosevelt, my fifth cousin once removed, asked me to marry him, though I was only nineteen, it seemed entirely natural and I never even thought that we were both young and inexperienced.

Later that fall, ecstatic, she wrote to him, " . . . I love you, dearest, and I hope that I shall always prove worthy of the love which you have given me. I have never known before what it was to be absolutely happy."

Eleanor signed her letters to him "Little Nell," the name she had used in letters to her father, signaling how completely she had given her heart to him. Franklin, in turn, sent her copies of his favorite poetry and, despite his rigorous college schedule in Cambridge, traveled often to New York to spend every hour he could with her.

However, the path to blissful marriage did not open up magically before them. Franklin was known for his easy banter, sometimes criticized for his tendency toward insincerity, and, as a result, even his own mother sometimes misread his deepest feelings. So when Franklin told his mother he had proposed to Eleanor, she suffered a considerable shock. Since her husband's death in 1900, she had built her life and dreams around her son. Now, suddenly, he had plans of his own, plans that would take him from her, plans she set all her influence firmly against. They were so young, she complained—he only 21 and she 19—there was time enough to consider marriage later. No doubt Sara Roosevelt had also hoped for a match, when the time did come, with someone more sophisticated, someone who would perhaps be a more likely asset to Franklin's future. She suggested they delay their announcement and proposed that Franklin should take a trip to Europe with her in the meantime, hoping this break would cool down youthful emotions and restore reason.

Finally, after consultations with both Eleanor and Franklin, Sara Roosevelt settled for a compromise. They would wait a year to announce their engagement, and instead of going so far, Franklin would sail with his mother to the West Indies for part of the winter while Eleanor remained in New York. But the winter passed, and neither of them changed their minds. Franklin could be stubborn and he was stubborn about Eleanor. Wedding plans were made.

When Franklin Roosevelt was born, James and Sara Roosevelt had asked Eleanor's father to be his godfather. Now Eleanor prepared to marry her father's godson, possibly hoping to recapture some of the happiness that she had felt with her father. But Franklin Roosevelt did not have her father's characteristics, and, in any case, her father had not been as constant and reliable as she tended to remember him being. As her longtime friend and biographer Joseph P. Lash has written, "In this inability to see the man she loved as he really was, she set the stage for much disappointment for herself." But Eleanor Roosevelt saw Franklin though the shining eyes of first love.

As if unconsciously foreshadowing a part of their own future, Eleanor and Franklin attended Theodore Roosevelt's presidential inauguration in Washington on March 5, 1905, less than two weeks before their wedding. Franklin, a Democrat, later explained that he had voted for his Republican relative because "I felt he was a better Democrat than the Democratic candidates." Eleanor recounted her recollection of the event: "Franklin and I went to our seats on the steps just back of Uncle Ted and his family. I was interested and excited, but politics still meant little to me . . . I told myself I had seen a historical event—and I never expected to see another inauguration in the family!"

The wedding of Franklin and Eleanor Roosevelt took place on her mother's birthday, March 17, 1905, in New York, in the home of Eleanor's cousin, Susie Parish. As the wedding hour approached, a hush came over the guests in the drawing room as they expectantly awaited the arrival of the president of the United States. Eleanor had arranged the wedding around her uncle's schedule (he would be in town to give a St. Patrick's Day speech) and had written him to ask "... do you think you could give me away?" It was a request her godfather joyfully honored. Just before three o'clock, the clatter of horse hooves signaled his arrival, and, bedecked with top hat and wearing a shamrock in his lapel, he vaulted from his open carriage and hurried upstairs, where Eleanor waited. Dressed in satin covered with the Brussels lace worn by her mother and Grandmother Hall, Eleanor approached the altar on the arm of her favorite uncle. There Franklin met her, and the two exchanged vows quietly before the gathering of friends and family. First congratulations came from the president, who quipped in his high-pitched voice, "Well, Franklin, there's nothing like keeping the name in the family." As Eleanor would note later with amusement, her uncle received considerably more attention at the reception afterward than did the bride and groom. At one point in the festivities, the young bride and groom found themselves standing completely alone in one room, while a peal of engaging laughter in the adjoining room signaled that Uncle Teddy had once again captivated an audience of enchanted listeners. Among the many congratulatory messages, a cable arrived that day from London. With just one word it wished them happiness: "Bonheur." It was signed, "Souvestre."

Franklin and Eleanor spent a brief honeymoon at Sara's home at Hyde Park in upstate New York, returning to the city to take up residence in an apartment while Franklin completed his graduate law studies at Columbia University. That summer they set out for their "real" honeymoon in Europe, where they traveled for three months from England to Paris and from Venice to the Italian Alps. Nearly everywhere they went, relatives or acquaintances were on hand to introduce them to society. But the best times they had were those they spent together, just the two of them. They delighted in showing each other their favorite haunts—Eleanor showing Franklin places she had visited with Mlle. Souvestre; Franklin introducing her to his favorite bookstore in London or to a choice café in Paris or Venice. In England, they visited Allenswood, but Marie Souvestre was gone. She had died of cancer on March 30, her wedding greeting to them among her last acts. Eleanor would keep the picture of her mentor on her bed stand for the rest of her life.

4

YOUNG WIFE, YOUNG MOTHER— THE EARLY YEARS 1905–1918

Eleanor and Franklin enjoyed their time together in Europe, but by the time they headed home in September, Eleanor had begun feeling quite ill. Always strong and healthy, she was both surprised and concerned by what for her was an unpleasant new experience. Once she arrived home in New York, however, she was overjoyed to learn that she was expecting a baby—she had been afraid she might never have children. The good news did not make her feel less miserable physically, though, and as it turned out, she would spend most of the next 10 years giving birth to six children. Despite discomfort that ranged from mild to intense during these years, Eleanor's strong sense of obligation and enormous energy drove her to continue her life as if she felt fine, meticulously keeping appointments and meeting responsibilities.

At the time, she never questioned this self-imposed credo of absolute discipline, although later she criticized what she came to see as youthful rigidity. "What it really does," she wrote, "is to kill a certain amount of the power of enjoyment. It makes one a stoic, but too much of a thing is as bad as too little, and I think it tends to make you draw away from other people and into yourself." She would struggle throughout her life to find the right balance between "too much" and "too little." She had seen the damage too little discipline could do, but was too young in these early years with Franklin to see that too much discipline could also do harm.

Eleanor and Franklin's first child was born May 3, 1906, and they named her Anna Eleanor Roosevelt, after Eleanor and Eleanor's mother. With the summer of 1906 came Eleanor's first season at Franklin's family's summer home on Campobello, an island off the coast of Maine. Franklin had grown up spending summers there, reveling in its natural beauty and bracing climate. He loved his yacht, the *Half Moon*, and relished piloting it through the narrow passageways amidst the challenges of fog and wayward breezes. Eleanor, who had survived an ocean vessel collision as a small child, was afraid of water, though she valiantly tried to fish with him. Franklin also enjoyed tennis, but Eleanor didn't play. So, aside from going on an occasional walk with Franklin and packing provisions for his sailing trips with friends, Eleanor participated little in the outdoor life her husband excelled in.

At Campobello, Sara was in charge, as she was at Hyde Park. Eleanor, who had gained so much independence and confidence during her years at Allenswood, had begun to lose ground rapidly. Overshadowed and outpaced by Franklin's domineering mother, Eleanor tried to accommodate and appease and smooth over. But she felt inadequate in every aspect of her marriage, in part because she was left with very little responsibility. Sara arranged for their living quarters, hired their servants and dictated much of their schedule. The couple had returned home from their honeymoon to a surprise—a new home at 125 East 36th Street, Sara's wedding present to them, complete with three servants and only three blocks from her own New York City place. For Christmas she gave them plans for adjoining houses she expected to build, "number and street not quite decided." The plans showed that sliding panels would enable the dining rooms and living rooms of the two houses to be joined. The houses were built at 47 and 49 East 65th Street, and in 1908 they all moved in—Franklin and Eleanor in one and Sara in the other—so she could move in and out of their lives at will.

Meanwhile, Franklin's career was moving along. He passed the bar in the spring of 1907, enabling him to practice law, a profession he did not, however, intend to pursue for a lifetime. It was his intention, he confidently announced to his colleagues, to run for political office and ultimately to become president of the United States. He planned, he said, to follow roughly the same prescription used with such success by his cousin Teddy: New York State assemblyman, assistant secretary of the navy, governor of New York, and then the White House. He had set his ambitions high, but not, he thought, unreasonably so.

The morning of December 23, 1907, Eleanor gave birth to their second child and first son, James, named after Franklin's father. Her dependency on nurses and servants to look after the children continued to haunt her, though. "I know now," Eleanor would write with wisdom acquired later, "that what we should have done was to have no servants those first few years; so I could have acquired knowledge and self-confidence and other people could not fool me about either the housework or the children."

Sara Roosevelt, overly helpful and intrusive, unwittingly taxed Eleanor's equanimity to the breaking point. But Eleanor, determined to be a model daughter-in-law and to keep her word that Sara would never regret Franklin's decision to marry her, struggled not to complain. However, more and more, Sara's daunting presence undercut her own opportunity to take charge and mature. The young couple lived near her house in New York; they spent their weekends at Hyde Park with her; and they spent their summers at Campobello, usually with Sara directing nearly every aspect of the summer activities. Sara arranged the flowers when the young Roosevelts had company, she entertained for them in her dining room and she handed out unending volumes of unasked-for domestic advice.

By the time the three moved into the adjacent houses on East 65th Street in the fall of 1908, Eleanor was close to a minor explosion. A few weeks after the move, Franklin found her crying bitterly as she sat at her dressing table. He asked what was wrong. She did not, she explained, like living in a house that she described as "not in any way mine, one that I had done nothing about and which did not represent the way I wanted to live." The moment passed, but the problem did not. Eleanor had begun to realize that she needed to transcend her tendency to absorb other people's personalities, and she needed to take initiative for developing her own tastes and for making her own decisions.

At the time of the move to the twin houses, Eleanor was already pregnant with their third child, and Sara spent evenings with her while Franklin was out on the town in New York, often returning home very late from poker games, dinners and events. Looking back on the early years of their marriage, Eleanor would later write: "I was always more comfortable with older people, and when I found myself with groups of young people I still felt inadequate. . . . I think I must have spoiled a good deal of fun for Franklin because of this inability to feel at ease . . ." As long as she could stay quietly at home, though, she made no objection to his more sociable activities.

On March 18, 1909, Franklin, Jr., was born. He was their second son, and, as Eleanor would later describe him, "the biggest and most beautiful of all the babies." She was very proud of him. But little Franklin, not as strong as he first appeared, had heart trouble. That fall, when all the children caught the flu, little Franklin became gravely ill. On November 27, only seven months and nine days after he was born, his weakened heart stopped beating. Eleanor was devastated. Sara wrote in her journal: "F. and E. are most wonderful, but poor E.'s mother heart is well nigh broken. She so hoped and cannot believe her baby is gone from her."

Eleanor grieved deeply and long, immersed in self-blame and sorrow. As she recalled in her autobiography:

> We took him to Hyde Park to bury him and, to this day, so many years later, I can stand by his tiny stone in the churchyard and see the little group of people gathered around his tiny coffin, and remember how cruel it seemed to leave him out there alone in the cold.
>
> I was young and morbid and reproached myself bitterly for having done so little about the care of this baby. I felt he had been left too much to the nurse, and I knew too little about him, and that in some way I must be to blame.

Eleanor recovered from this blow only gradually, and, deeply afflicted, she visited the churchyard often, carrying flowers to the bleak little grave. She had suffered painful losses before as a child, and death was no stranger to her. Yet she continued to punish herself with blame for many months, struggling to overcome this further deep erosion of her self-confidence as a mother and as a woman. While others saw her as the ideal wife and mother, she could not shake off her self-doubts and withdrawn moods. Her husband, to whom all this was alien, hoped she would heal herself and tried to leave her space to recover.

By the following year, Franklin began moving toward the political career that beckoned to him, as he prepared to campaign for the office of New York state senator from the district in which Hyde Park was located. Eleanor was supportive in spirit but still grieved for little Franklin and remained more

Eleanor and Franklin in 1910. (Franklin D. Roosevelt Library)

focused on family concerns: She was pregnant again and more concerned than ever about the health of the child she was carrying. That summer she would leave Campobello earlier than usual to return to New York for Elliott's birth, which came September 23, 1910. In these early years, as she later wrote, "It never occurred to me that I had any part to play" in Franklin's political ambitions, and she participated very little. She recalled that he waged an unusually aggressive campaign for the time, visiting every town, village and corner store, speaking personally to every voter he could. During the campaign, Eleanor recalls, he was "thin, . . . high-strung, and at times nervous. . . . No lines as yet in his face, but at times a set look of his jaw denoted that this apparently pliable youth [he was 28] had strength and Dutch obstinacy in his make-up." He was persuasive, had charisma and attracted voters and he won, though by a narrow margin: 15,708 to 14,568. It was the first time in more than a quarter century that a Democrat had carried the district. Franklin's political career had begun.

Franklin's election meant that the family would move to Albany, where they found a house on State Street, while they rented out their place in New York City. After the reception held in their new residence on January 1, Eleanor quickly organized the servants to put the house in order. "I have always had a passion for being completely settled as quickly as possible," she recalled, "wherever I lived. I want all my photographs hung, all my ornaments out, and everything in order within the first twenty-four hours. Dirt and disorder make me positively uncomfortable."

These years in Albany proved to be an important time: Sara would not be there to turn to for advice or help. Now at last Eleanor had a chance to do things on her own. "I had to stand on my own feet now and I wanted to be independent," she wrote. "I was beginning to realize that something within me craved to be an individual."

That winter Eleanor and Franklin found out that James had a heart murmur, and the fear of losing another child haunted Eleanor once again. All winter they carried the little three-year-old up and down the stairs in the Albany house rather than risk any strain on his heart. The memory of little Franklin lingered still. But in Albany, for the first time since her days working with the children in Rivington Street,

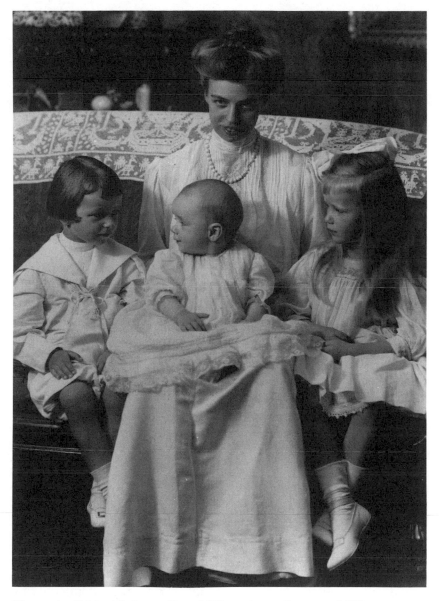

Eleanor in 1911 with three of her children, Anna, James and Elliott. (Franklin D. Roosevelt Library)

Eleanor began to extend her interests beyond her family. Partly as a gesture of support for Franklin, she began to pay daily visits to the state legislature to sit in the public gallery during morning sessions. She enjoyed watching the personalities at work, following the arguments and the methods of persuasion—and she found the proceedings stimulating and absorbing. In the afternoons, she returned home to be with her children, but her political education had begun.

During this time she also caught a glimpse of the underbelly of politics when a country newspaper was forced out of business for supporting her husband in a fight against the Tammany Hall bloc from New York City. Known for its political abuses, the Tammany segment of the Democratic Party often played dirty, and this time people who had sided with Roosevelt got caught in the cross fire. Eleanor became outraged at the injustice. Public service, she realized for the first time, could have its ugly, dangerous side, especially for those who were not financially independent.

During his second year in Albany, Franklin came out in favor of women's right to vote—a hot issue in 1912. But Eleanor, surprisingly, had not ever given the cause much thought. Raised with Victorian values, she didn't question the assumption, despite Mlle. Souvestre's influence, that men were naturally superior and that politics should be left to them. As she later confessed, " . . . while I realized that if my husband was a suffragist I probably must be, too, I cannot claim to have been a feminist in those early days."

Now an old hand at the Albany scene, Eleanor began to seek out the wives of new assemblymen and journalists to make them feel more welcome and at ease. When Franklin and his political allies needed a place to discuss issues and plan strategies, she found herself easily making their home a hub for afternoon gatherings, dinners and late-night sessions. In Albany, she found herself exposed, for the first time, to a wide range of people, and she found she liked it. "I was not a snob," she later remarked, "largely because I never really thought about why you asked people to your house or claimed them as friends. Anyone who came was grist to my mill, because I was beginning to get interested in human beings, and I found that almost everyone had something interesting to contribute to my education." It was a premise that would remain a cornerstone of her philosophy for the rest of her life.

As the presidential campaign of 1912 developed, the political situation became complicated when Teddy Roosevelt threw a wrench into Republican plans by forming a new party, the

Progressive, or Bull Moose, Party. Then, as the Progressive nominee, he went after the presidency in opposition to his old friend, incumbent President William Howard Taft, thereby splitting the Republicans' vote and weakening their position. It was a controversial move.

Franklin, meanwhile, campaigned hard for Woodrow Wilson's nomination by the Democrats, becoming recognized as Wilson's top supporter in upstate New York. Enthusiastic about the prospects of his candidate, Franklin took Eleanor to the Democratic National Convention in Baltimore that summer, and she found herself caught up by the excitement, though put off by the demonstrations and hoopla. Yet she still was not really involved, and before the conclusion, she left Franklin to his meetings and took the children to Campobello. There, a few days later, she received a cryptic telegram from her husband:

> MRS. F.D. ROOSEVELT
> CAMPOBELLO EASTPORT MAINE
> WILSON NOMINATED THIS AFTERNOON   ALL MY
> PLANS VAGUE   SPLENDID TRIUMPH   FRANKLIN.

Franklin had a campaign of his own to wage that year for his second term in the state senate, but he fell ill suddenly with a debilitating but mild case of typhoid fever—which Eleanor had also caught but recovered from quickly. While Eleanor looked after him, his friend Louis Howe, a seasoned Albany journalist, campaigned for him in upstate New York. Howe felt sure he saw presidential material in Franklin, and he combined his own political savvy with Franklin's growing stature to good advantage. Franklin won. But he wouldn't spend long in Albany this term, since Wilson also won, and Franklin's own share of the "splendid triumph" began to pay off. On March 13, 1913—the day of the inauguration—the offer came. Would Franklin accept the position of assistant secretary of the navy, he was asked—the very position that had led his cousin Teddy toward the presidency! With a verbal tip of the hat to his heroic, blustery relative, Franklin replied without hesitation, "I'd like it bully well."

The Roosevelts were on their way to Washington. For Eleanor, that meant dismantling her household and gathering up her children and servants, organizing their belongings and marshaling another move. But she was used to it by now, a veteran at organizing her "army on the move," as she liked to say, from household to household, from New York City to Albany to Hyde Park to Campobello. This time was no different.

But life in Washington would be different. For Eleanor, life in the nation's capital became a whirl of social obligations. She spent her days calling on wives of dignitaries (60 calls her first week in town), her evenings dining out with Franklin and his Washington contacts. Once a week, a group of political allies gathered at the Roosevelts' house for dinner and discussions.

As wife of the new assistant secretary of the navy, she became determined to learn navy protocol and master the art of fitting into the ceremonies surrounding her husband's ship inspections. And she showed pluck. Invited to board the battleship *Rhode Island* to view the navy at target practice, she was asked by a young officer if she would like to view the proceedings from atop the skeleton mast. So she pulled on trousers and climbed the dizzying distance to the top of the mast. "None of the other women seemed willing to risk climbing the mast," one of the ship's officers declared, clearly impressed.

Her old shyness faded away. As Roosevelts, she and Franklin were seen as representative of the best of Theodore Roosevelt's Progressive Party policies as well as Wilson's new order—and the call for social change that both camps represented. They made a striking couple. One society matron remarked that the Franklin Roosevelts were, in her opinion, "the most attractive and nicest young couple I know."

During the years that Franklin was assistant secretary of the navy, the Roosevelts had two more children: the second Franklin, Jr., born August 17, 1914, and the sixth and last child, John Aspinwall (named after Franklin's uncle), born March 13, 1916.

Franklin, Jr., came while his father was making a bid for the Democratic nomination for senator of New York State. The baby, which was due on the 26th, arrived early, but luckily Franklin had come early to Campobello to be with Eleanor, despite the campaign. Once he knew mother and child were well, he left again to garner votes in the primary election. He lost the nomination, however, and returned to his Navy Department post in Washington.

Already by 1913, Eleanor had found she was juggling so much that she hired a young woman, Lucy Mercer, as her personal secretary. Lucy helped out in the household with correspondence, with the children and filling in wherever she was needed. Her family had a fine social standing, and she had exquisite manners, so if an extra guest was needed to round out a dinner party, Eleanor invited Lucy. She was 22 at the time, tall and beautiful, and her engaging smile won over the whole family, including Sara, ever influential, even from New York. Eleanor came to rely extensively on her new secretary.

During the summer of 1914, war broke out in Europe between the Allies, led by England and France, and the Central Powers, led by Germany. Initially, the United States tried to maintain neutrality, but as the months of 1914, 1915 and 1916 wore on, attacks on American ships by German submarines battered Wilson's commitment to neutrality, and finally the United States entered the war on the side of the Allies on April 6, 1917.

"It's not an army we must shape and train for war," Wilson intoned, "it is the nation." All citizens, including noncombatants, were urged to do their share, and Eleanor enthusiastically pitched in.

She began by ending her routine of social calls. Soon, having never before used a sewing machine, she was sewing pajamas for the Red Cross. She resolved to learn to drive, a small salvo for independence, and her war work became an even more radical strike for independence. She often set off as early as five A.M. for the Red Cross canteens where volunteers prepared soup, coffee and sandwiches for troops waiting in trains in the Washington railroad yards—sometimes as many as 10 trainloads a day. Eleanor, who was generally considered the canteen "dynamo," was a whiz at making change quickly and accurately and designed the canteen's accounting system, an especially admirable feat for a woman who at one time had no idea how to keep her household books.

She also gave out wool to knitters and collected the products once they were finished. Later she took charge of the knitting at the Navy Department, supervising more than 40 units. Soon she found herself presiding at rallies, and making speeches.

She did everything that was asked of her with vigor and determination. As described by Sara's sister, who lived in Washington, "Eleanor is the 'willing horse' and they call upon her at all hours, all the time." In May 1918, the Red Cross even suggested that Eleanor go to England to organize a canteen there, but Eleanor felt she had to stay home with her family. Yet, she was tempted, writing Sara: " . . . one really can't help wanting to do the real thing instead of playing at it over here."

Franklin was ordered to the front in Europe in July 1918 to inspect operations there and report on the needs of American bases and ships. Influenza had become pandemic by August; 69,000 American troops had fallen ill. (From 1918 to 1919, the deadly influenza strain, often turning into pneumonia, would sweep throughout the world, killing between 15 million and 25 million people.)

That summer, Eleanor stayed in Washington during the month of July, despite the heat, having sent her children to stay with their grandmother at Hyde Park. "It was not an unusual thing for me to work from nine in the morning until one or two the next morning," she wrote, "and be back again by ten. The nights were hot [unrelieved by air conditioning] and it was possible to sleep only if you were exhausted."

From Paris, Franklin wrote in September that he was ill. How ill only became apparent upon his return, when Eleanor was asked to meet the docking of his vessel, the *Leviathan*, with a doctor and ambulance, and Franklin was carried off the ship on a stretcher. He had double pneumonia.

5

CHANGING COURSE IN A SHIFTING WIND 1918–1932

Franklin recovered from his pneumonia, but a greater trauma was in store for Eleanor. While unpacking Franklin's baggage, she came across a packet of letters from her secretary, Lucy Mercer. They were undeniably love letters. "The bottom dropped out of my own particular world," she would later recall, "and I faced myself, my surroundings, my world, honestly for the first time."

Always insecure, Eleanor now suddenly doubted that Franklin had ever really loved her. She was certain he could have no feelings for her now. Disheartened, Eleanor inventoried what she saw as her shortcomings—her wide mouth and protruding teeth; her unfashionable height, approaching 6 feet; her high, shrill voice; disappearing chin. She knew her serious manner and despondent moods poorly matched Franklin's light-hearted, fun-loving nature. Moreover, having borne six children, she had established separate bedrooms at Hyde Park and in Washington—abstinence was the best birth control method she knew. She had what she admitted was a more somber, less frivolous approach to life than his. Lucy Mercer was prettier and younger. She was probably more fun to be with, a pleasant companion with a low, sexy voice and that charming, engaging smile everyone loved. Now Eleanor felt unlovely and unloved.

In the days that followed, she moved like a stricken woman, her face bleached to a gray pallor. She lost weight. Franklin, on whose love she had depended as she had on her father's, had, like her father, let her down.

There was no turning back. She had to confront Franklin with the evidence. She would give him his freedom; if he wanted a divorce, she would not stand in his way. Franklin's mother was outraged, however, at the thought, informing him that if he divorced Eleanor he would not receive another dollar from her. Louis Howe warned that divorce would ruin Franklin's political career, and Franklin recognized that even his position with the Navy Department would be jeopardized. Still, he may have been tempted to give up his wife, children, inheritance, career and job to flee into Lucy's arms. But Lucy Mercer, a Catholic, could not envision marrying a divorced man. Louis Howe stepped in as a go-between, pleading with Eleanor to forgive Franklin, begging Franklin to think of his future. In the end they were convinced.

But this was a watershed in their marriage, and nothing after this incident was ever the same. Franklin promised to break off his affair with Lucy, and he and Eleanor worked to form a new partnership. The changes came gradually, however, and while much affection between them continued, for Eleanor, the trust she had once felt was gone and physical intimacy was out of the question. Eleanor began building a new independence, both personal and financial, and during the years to come, she began to realize that her personal fulfillment could not depend on Franklin or anyone but herself. From wisdom gained from these experiences, came her most often quoted comment, "No one can make you feel inferior without your consent." She successfully channeled the loneliness, disappointment and loss of intimacy with Franklin into other outlets, including social reform and political activity. But the personal wound she felt never healed completely. She is said to have confided years later to close friends, "I have the memory of an elephant. I can forgive, but I cannot forget." Determined to make the new partnership work, Franklin worked hard to please Eleanor. He attended church and spent more time with the children. For her part, she began to go to parties she would have shunned before, and to her surprise she began to enjoy them. They worked together editing his diary of his European trip.

The war drew to a close in November 1918, and Franklin convinced the secretary of the navy that he should be sent to Europe to oversee the liquidation of U.S. naval establishments there and that Eleanor should go with him. They set sail in January 1919. At 34, this was her first return to Europe since their honeymoon in 1905. She was outgoing, active and involved. Europe showed the impact of a devastating war: 8.5 million soldiers dead and 20 million wounded. "Every other woman wears a crepe veil to her knees," wrote Eleanor. And later, "The streets are all clear, all is neat and clean but you feel as though ghosts were beside you." While they were there, Woodrow Wilson was battling for his Fourteen Points at the Paris Peace Conference, and they returned home aboard the same ship with the Wilsons. Wilson was hopeful for success. Congress, however, would oppose the treaty that Wilson had fought so hard for at the conference table, and never did ratify it, primarily because of the inclusion of the formation of that forerunner of the United Nations, the League of Nations. As an alliance to promote international cooperation and peace it was a concept feared and resisted by many Americans at the time because the league seemed to represent a loss of national independence and autonomy.

The Democratic National Convention of 1920 was held in July in San Francisco, and when Franklin headed off to the convention, Eleanor took the children to Campobello. There a telegram arrived from Josephus Daniels, the secretary of the navy. Franklin had been nominated for vice president on a ticket headed by presidential candidate James M. Cox, governor of Ohio. "I was glad for my husband," Eleanor wrote, "but it never occurred to me to be very much excited."

She did, however, accompany him on a four-week whistle-stop campaign from New York to Colorado, and during the trip she began to gain a new respect for Louis Howe. When she'd first met Howe in Albany, she had never cared much for him. He was a curiously gnomelike man, who, as Eleanor described him, "was entirely indifferent to his appearance; he not only neglected his clothes but gave the impression at times that cleanliness was not of particular interest to him. The fact [was] that he had rather extraordinary eyes and a fine mind I was fool enough not to have discovered as yet, and it was by externals alone that I had judged him in our association prior to this trip.

"In later years," she continued, "I learned that he had always liked me and thought I was worth educating, and for that reason he made an effort on this trip to get to know me. . . ." Caught in the spell of Louis Howe's enthusiasm and knowledge, she began to take more interest in politics.

But Cox was little known, the Democrats focused on Wilson's unpopular campaign to join the League of Nations, and they lost this round to the Republican candidate, Warren G. Harding. With the change of guard in the White House, Franklin also lost his position as assistant secretary of the navy, and for the first time in a decade, Franklin held no political office. The Roosevelts left Washington for New York, where Franklin joined a law firm and began planning the next stage in his political career.

The prospect of living in New York—with none of the responsibilities she slowly had come to enjoy—did not entice Eleanor. "I did not look forward to a winter of four days a week in New York with nothing but teas and luncheons and dinners to take up my time," she recalled. So she took up cooking, preparing a meal twice a week for practice for the family of a former professional cook, and enrolled in a business school to study typing and shorthand.

For Eleanor, as she settled into her New York City life, the most important event for her continuing political education was a visit paid her by Mrs. Frank Vanderlip, chair of the League of Women Voters for New York State. On August 26, the 19th Amendment to the Constitution had been enacted, giving women the right to vote, and that same year, to educate women in the ways of politics, a new organization was formed: the League of Women Voters. Would Mrs. Roosevelt be willing to serve on the board and present the league with reports on current national legislation, Mrs. Vanderlip wanted to know. Eleanor hesitated. She was interested, she explained, but had no particular familiarity with bills before Congress in Washington. Although she certainly had listened to many conversations on the subject, she didn't feel qualified for the job. But, the league's chair argued, Eleanor was probably more conversant than even the most knowledgeable women in New York

City. Furthermore, she would have help; Elizabeth Read, an intelligent, able attorney, would serve as a resource and would mark the bills in the Congressional Record that would interest the league. Finally, Eleanor agreed and began spending one morning a week at Elizabeth Read's office, studying legislation. Those bills that needed further study came home with her, and the league began to profit from her monthly reports.

Read soon became a close ally and friend. "I liked her at once," wrote Eleanor, "and she gave me a sense of confidence." Eleanor also soon met Elizabeth's friend, Esther Lape, with whom Elizabeth shared a house in Greenwich Village. Esther, a Wellesley graduate who had taught English at Swarthmore and Barnard Colleges, "had a brilliant mind and a driving force, a kind of nervous power," according to Eleanor. "Elizabeth seemed calmer, more practical and domestic, but I came to see that hers was a keen and analytical mind in its way as brilliant as Esther's."

Eleanor had little time left for many of her old routines from earlier days in New York. "My mother-in-law," she said, "was distressed because I was not always available, as I had been when I lived in New York before." But this, Eleanor felt, was for the best. ". . . I was thinking things out for myself and becoming an individual. Had I never done this, perhaps I might have been saved some difficult experiences, but I have never regretted even my mistakes. They all added to my understanding of other human beings, and I came out in the end a more tolerant, understanding and charitable person."

The summer of 1921, after concluding his business in New York, Franklin joined Eleanor, Sara and the children at Campobello, as usual. Franklin had bought a small sailboat, the *Vireo*, to teach the boys sailing, and on August 10, he took the family out on a jaunt. After a fine outing, as they headed back toward home, they caught sight of a forest fire burning wildly and immediately made for shore to help put it out, the boys and Franklin splashing through the water in their eagerness. Once that good deed was done, they struck out for home again, arriving about four o'clock in the afternoon. Franklin decided to go for a dip in the inland lake on the far side of the island, returning home and taking another quick plunge in the icy Bay of Fundy on the way, before loping up to the house. Dried off by his run, he stopped to look through his mail before going on into his bedroom to change clothes for dinner. By this time, though, he'd begun to feel a slight chill and changed his mind, deciding to turn in early instead, since he'd been going nonstop for days before. No one thought anything of it.

But the next day, Franklin was running a fever, and Eleanor became concerned. She called the local doctor, who diagnosed the ailment as a bad cold. But it soon became apparent that the problem was far more serious. His temperature rose to 102 degrees, and he had pain in his back and his legs. When Franklin tried to get up, his left leg dragged strangely and wouldn't take his weight. Paralysis had set in, and after consultations it became apparent that Franklin had come down with infantile paralysis, or poliomyelitis (polio), as it's more often called today. Although he didn't accept the verdict immediately, he would never stand or walk on his own again, and the only sports that remained to the once-active athlete were swimming and water polo.

Caused by a virus that was not yet isolated or identified in 1921, polio had been around for centuries, but it only recently had become a widespread killer and crippler, reaching epidemic proportions in the United States in the early years of the 20th century. In New York City alone, 9,000 cases occurred in 1916, with 27,000 cases across the nation. Panic set in, and people fled from the cities in the summer, when the epidemics seemed to hit. There was no vaccine available in those days, and there was no known effective treatment. All a doctor could do was let the disease run its course, try to make the patient comfortable and then attempt to rehabilitate the severely damaged nerves and flaccid muscles.

Franklin's family called in the foremost polio specialist, Dr. Robert Lovett, who came to Campobello to examine him, but the prognosis was not good. Franklin was still running a temperature of 100 degrees, and he was completely paralyzed—now in both legs—from his waist down, his facial muscles also somewhat affected and his back muscles so weak that he couldn't come to a sitting position without help. He was transferred from Campobello to New York by boat and train and entered Presbyterian Hospital, where he stayed until the end of October, when he had finally recovered sufficiently to go home to the town house on 65th Street.

A daily regimen of agonizing and strenuous rehabilitation exercises followed but produced little change. Once so able and athletic, Franklin now was virtually helpless. Eleanor planned her days to spend every afternoon taking care of him, when the nurse wasn't there. His pain and frustration, coupled with his effort to maintain an optimistic, cheerful attitude began to win her sympathy. He was determined not to give up.

Sara, however, had come to the conclusion that her son was going to be an invalid for the rest of his life. Convinced that his friend and political consultant Louis Howe and Eleanor were demanding too much of him, Sara began planning his permanent retirement to Hyde Park, a plan Eleanor ardently opposed.

It was a trying winter for Eleanor. The house on 65th Street was crowded. They had put Franklin in the back bedroom on the third floor, where it was quiet. Anna and Elliott had the two small rooms on the fourth floor, and Eleanor invited Howe to stay in the large front bedroom on the third floor, which was used by the nurse during the day, while he was at his office downtown. This way Howe had a place to stay, which he needed, and he was on hand in the evenings to make plans and encourage Franklin. The connecting doors on the fourth floor made it possible for the two little boys and their nurse to use rooms on the top floor of Sara's adjoining house, and Eleanor slept on a cot in one of their rooms.

At every turn, Sara took Eleanor to task over Franklin's care. Fearful that he would become overtired, she insisted he should be kept completely quiet at all times, which was completely contrary to the regimen of exercise and stimulation that his doctors had prescribed. As always, Sara was certain that she was right—particularly where her only child was con-cerned—and long and bitter disagreements ensued.

The strain finally got to Eleanor, who typically kept her emotions carefully under check until, as she would later re-count:

> . . . one afternoon in the spring, when I was trying to read to the two youngest boys, I suddenly found myself sobbing as I read. I could not think why I was sobbing, nor could I stop. Elliott came in from school, dashed in to look at me and fled. Mr. Howe came in and tried to find out what the matter was, but he gave it up as a bad job. The two little

> boys went off to bed and I sat on the sofa in the sitting room
> and sobbed and sobbed.

Finally, too proud to keep up this out-of-character behavior, she sought out an empty room in her mother-in-law's house, poured cold water on her face, and regained her composure, and she never recalled losing control in that way again.

By spring, Franklin was able to sit on the floor and play with the little boys, who were barely aware there was anything wrong, their father was able to move his upper torso so naturally, and his attitude was so lacking in self-pity. Eleanor felt that Franklin had been affected for the better psychologically by this tragedy—he had become less judgmental and more patient. Other observers found that he listened, whereas as a young senator in Albany, he had always been in too big a hurry, too certain he already knew the answers.

"Franklin's illness proved a blessing in disguise," Eleanor later wrote with characteristic affirmation, "for it gave him strength and courage he had not had before. He had to think out the fundamentals of living and learn the greatest of all lessons—infinite patience and never-ending persistence." His illness also made him need her in a way he never had before, and this must have given her some satisfaction.

That summer, Eleanor began to realize that her boys would never again have the companionship of their father teaching them to swim or camping or fishing and boating with them, and she resolved she would have to try to fill in. Though afraid of water, she learned to swim at the YWCA, took them camping and relearned horseback riding to fill in for their father as well as she could.

Franklin's doctor, meanwhile, maintained that the best medicine for Franklin would be to plunge back into as active a life as he could sustain, and Howe was quick to encourage him to think again about the political career he had begun. He also began to press Eleanor to begin making contacts and to think actively about ways to keep the Roosevelt name in the public awareness.

Louis Howe continued to play a key role in Eleanor's political education. He insisted that, if Franklin was ever to return to politics, Eleanor would have to keep the Roosevelt name alive while he recuperated. He taught her public speaking. He built her confidence and helped her develop a public presence. He tutored her in the intricacies of political campaigning, and he pushed her to join the Women's Division of the State Democratic Committee. Eleanor would later comment, "This little man was really the biggest man from the point of view of imagination and determination I have ever known."

Dating back to her days as a member of the Junior League working in the Rivington Street project in New York, Eleanor had become an advocate of reform, and she began to see that reform could spring most readily from political power. When the 19th Amendment was enacted in 1920, she saw her activism as the natural extension of the new rights and responsibilities she now had as a voting woman. In 1922, Eleanor met Marion Dickerman and her friend Nancy Cook, who invited her to preside at a luncheon to raise funds for the Women's Division of the State Democratic Committee. These were the first real contacts of the kind Howe had hoped she might make.

Eleanor, clearly at ease and comfortable, with her friends Peggy Levenson, Marion Dickerman's sister (left), Nancy Cook (second from left) and Marion Dickerman (right). (Franklin D. Roosevelt Library)

Marion Dickerman was tall and soft-spoken, a scholar with a dry wit, who taught and was vice principal at Todhunter, an exclusive girls' school in Manhattan. Nancy Cook, who lived with Marion, was a feminist and women's rights worker. The three women immediately took a liking to each other, and so began a warm and lasting friendship among the three of them. Franklin liked the two women Eleanor brought home—they were intelligent, energetic and politically savvy. Sara, however, did not. She disliked their mannish style of dress—often wearing vests, jackets and ties with knickerbockers (knickers), their hair short and curly—and she made them uncomfortable when they came to visit at Hyde Park. Eleanor's cousin, Alice Roosevelt Longworth, referred to them derisively as Eleanor's "female impersonators."

For Eleanor, though, this was the first time since she had attended Marie Souvestre's school that she felt at home and accepted as part of a community. Marion Dickerman and Nancy Cook were activists, and they introduced Eleanor to the world of labor issues such as the abolition of child labor, establishment of a minimum wage and a 48-hour workweek. They got her into the Women's Trade Union League, and they soon had her holding classes for working women in the basement of the 65th Street brownstone. Newspapers were attracted by her name and began quoting her on women's issues, and the "three musketeers," as they called themselves, began touring the state in a green Buick, campaigning to encourage women to vote for the Democratic side of the issues and candidates.

In 1924, Al Smith—then governor of New York—needed a young politician of stature to nominate him for president, and he tapped Eleanor's husband. It was Franklin's first public appearance since his illness, and Louis and Eleanor orchestrated it carefully. The event went smoothly, and it looked like Eleanor's work was beginning to pay off for Franklin, although, unfortunately, his candidate didn't win the nomination.

When Al Smith's national hopes were dashed, he turned to his campaign for the governorship of New York, in which Eleanor became especially active. Keeping communications open between her husband and the candidate, she frequently acted as the go-between. She often invited guests to dinner

FDR at Hyde Park in August 1924, with Democratic presidential nominee John W. Davis. (Photo World, Inc.)

whose wide-ranging interests provoked lively conversation, and politics became a frequent topic at their table.

From 1924 to 1928, Eleanor was the finance chair of the Women's Division of the State Democratic Committee in New York. When in 1928 the Democratic Party in New York began publishing the *Women's Democratic News*, they named Eleanor as editor. She also took on the job of advertising manager, and Louis Howe helped her learn page layout and advised her on headlines. Then, ascending swiftly to leadership, she was soon appointed chair of the Women's Platform Committee for the national Democratic Party. Eleanor initially became involved in political causes to help her husband—as a sort of stand-in for him as he recovered from his illness—but principles of her own now began to take shape. She was soon recognized for her honesty and vitality. She worked hard, never too proud to do whatever menial tasks needed to be done, and people saw her as fair-minded and dedicated.

At the end of the summer of 1924, Franklin, Eleanor and her friends Nancy and Marion were enjoying the last picnic of the season by Val-Kill Creek in a lovely wooded area about two miles from the main house at Hyde Park. It was a beautiful day, and it seemed a shame to have to call it quits for the season, just because Sara always closed Hyde Park for the winter. Why not build a cottage on the land there? Franklin volunteered. Then the three of them could come there any time of year. As it happened he owned a perfect plot on Val-Kill Creek, even though his mother owned most of the estate. He would happily let the three of them build on it.

The idea quickly caught fire. Excited by the idea, Franklin helped design the stone cottage, appointed himself contractor and builder and talked over every detail with its architect, Henry Toombs. Val-Kill Cottage opened New Year's Day 1926, and it became the home of Marion Dickerman and Nancy Cook and Eleanor's home away from home, a hideaway where she could just be herself and entertain her friends, away from the critical eyes of her mother-in-law.

That same year Franklin fell in love with a run-down resort in Warm Springs, Georgia. The warm mineral waters seemed soothing to his wasted leg muscles, and he hoped to find a cure. Envisioning a spa where people could come for rehabilitation from polio and similar muscular problems, he purchased the

In 1927, Eleanor and her friends built this stucco building to house the Val-Kill furniture factory. (Photograph taken in 1962). (Franklin D. Roosevelt Library)

property and began spending winter vacations there, where the warmer weather was easier on him. He brought sick and paralyzed people there, from all walks of life, to enjoy the warm waters, and he enjoyed trying to do something for them, always hoping—though nothing ever came of his hopes—that the waters would do more than just soothe. Eleanor occasionally went there with him, but for the most part, this was his own retreat. So, in a way, Eleanor and Franklin both found communities that fit their individual needs. Eleanor loved Val-Kill, with its commanding views of the rolling hills of Hyde Park, its large pond and its rock pool designed to look like a swimming hole. Val-Kill became Eleanor's home—the first home of her own she had ever had.

Sara found the new order of things unsettling, as her daughter-in-law slipped away from her control. "Can you tell me *why* Eleanor wants to go over to Val-Kill cottage to sleep every night?" she once asked a friend of Eleanor's. "Why doesn't she sleep here? This is her home. She belongs here."

The place became almost like a clubhouse for the "three musketeers." Nancy, a fine cabinetmaker, constructed much of the furniture, and Eleanor crocheted doilies decorated with their entwined monograms, EMN.

Inspired by Cook's furniture for the cottage, Eleanor, Nancy and Marion decided to start a furniture factory at Val-Kill in 1926. "Nancy Cook," as Eleanor described her, "was an attractive woman who could do almost anything with her hands." The three conceived the idea of manufacturing furniture in the Early American traditional style, using machine manufacturing techniques for the early stages of construction, but the old techniques of hand finishing for the final touches. They researched styles and techniques with the help of the Metropolitan Museum, the Hartford Museum and various historians and set up shop. The resulting fine furniture, because it was finished by hand, had the look and feel of antique wood, with the fine patina and sheen usually obtained only through years of use.

Franklin was interested in the enterprise because he saw it as a model that farmers might follow for producing income during slack seasons, without abandoning their farms. He hoped that the Val-Kill factory might serve as a training and employment site for young men in the area.

Eleanor provided most of the capital, partly from her earnings from radio appearances and writing, and partly from the nest egg left her by her parents. Nancy ran the enterprise.

At Marion's suggestion, Eleanor began teaching in New York City two and a half days a week at Todhunter, the private primary and secondary school for girls where Marion taught. Eleanor preferred teaching the older girls—16- and 17-year-olds—and she conducted classes in American history, English and American literature and later in current events. As always, she threw herself into the enterprise with gusto, and her students loved it. Eager to show her students the heartbeat of the city government and how it related to the lives it touched, she took them to see courts in session, to visit tenements (with their parents' permission) and market places. Later, she and Marion had an opportunity to buy the school, and they went in on it together.

In 1928, Al Smith and other Democratic Party leaders succeeded in luring Franklin back into politics, suggesting that he run for governor of New York while Smith ran again for president. Still paralyzed from the waist down, Franklin was otherwise a robust, healthy man. But he couldn't walk or stand without support, and he wore braces of leather and steel that locked at the knee to keep his legs from collapsing under him. However, although he had been out of politics for eight years, voters found him self-assured and intuitive if sometimes vague. As in his previous campaigns, he exhibited considerable charm and vitality, and he won. Al Smith, however, lost yet another bid for the White House.

As the Roosevelts headed once again for Albany, Eleanor realized she would have to give up her positions in the Democratic Party. As the governor's wife, her assertions could be too easily mistaken as being her husband's. But she loved teaching too much to give that up, even from Albany. Eleanor worked out a routine of leaving Albany for New York City each Sunday night by train to teach her classes. She then would return to Albany each Wednesday afternoon, usually correcting homework as she rode.

At this point, Eleanor couldn't juggle everything, and she hired a secretary, Malvina Thompson—dubbed "Tommy" by the children—whose crusty, honest approach to life made her a trusted, much loved member of Eleanor's newly extended family. Tommy would become Eleanor's reliable right hand and trusted ally throughout much of the challenging journey that lay before her.

Also with the move to Albany, Franklin hired a state trooper, a man named Earl Miller, as a bodyguard for Eleanor. Because Eleanor preferred to drive herself, rather than be chauffeured in a state car, Franklin felt that she needed protection. Earl was not well-educated but he was quick thinking and loyal, and he was very fond of Eleanor and she of him. She enjoyed his company, and as one friend put it, he became like a son to her. Rumors flew about the unusual closeness between them, but Eleanor and Earl never took this gossip seriously.

In 1930, Franklin ran again for governor, gaining an enormous victory, the result of a plurality of 725,000 over his Republican opponent, Charles H. Tuttle. It was the first time in the 20th century that any Democratic candidate had won the vote in all 52 counties of the state outside New York City. To Louis Howe and Franklin's other political advisers, the mandate placed Franklin clearly in line for a strong presidential campaign in 1932, the direction in which he was undeniably headed.

For Eleanor, these years in Albany "cast their shadow before them," as she put it, preparing the Roosevelts in a sort of dress rehearsal for the White House years to come.

6

THE CAMPAIGN AND THE EARLY WHITE HOUSE YEARS 1932–1936

They called it "Black Tuesday," and it was the most cata-strophic day in the history of the New York Stock Ex-change. In the course of one day, on October 29, 1929, the Dow Jones Industrial Average veered downward 30.57 points in the blackest moment in the history of Wall Street. Many investors, both large and small, lost heavily, as speculators were forced to sell at a loss and nearly $30 billion dollars disappeared. By the end of the day, investors had lost a sum almost equal to America's monetary losses during the war years 1914–18, and on the heels of the crash (though debatably not because of it) began a decade of unprecedented economic depression, a period so long and severe it became known as the Great Depression.

By 1932, unemployment had reached more than 29.4 per-cent, with nearly 11.5 million Americans out of work, and the numbers were still increasing. (In 1926, by contrast, the unem-ployment rate had been only 1 percent). The banking system was in a state of collapse. Prices and output had both dipped to only one-third of the levels in 1929. By 1932, the problem was not just a national problem, it had become an international problem, with 30 million people out of work worldwide, but the effect on the American people was also massive: Youth, minorities and the elderly were among the hardest hit. Unemployment for as long as a year or more frequently wiped out the entire accumulated wealth of a family, destroyed mental stability and family bonds and permanently derailed the career and educational plans of the younger generation.

This was the economic and political climate into which Franklin Delano Roosevelt cast his bid for presidential candidacy in 1932, and in one sense, it was a climate of opportunity: People were ready for a change. Franklin D. Roosevelt was a Democrat while Herbert Hoover, the incumbent presidential candidate who had presided over these years of bitter destitution, was a Republican.

In 1932, another factor had also become important for the first time in a presidential election: the women's vote. In part because of this fact, Eleanor began to campaign at her husband's side, touring the country with him at least part of the

Eleanor (left) whistle-stop campaigning with Franklin in 1932. (Franklin D. Roosevelt Library)

time as his campaign train paused for speeches at every whis- tle-stop. She was the first wife of a presidential candidate to do so.

As Franklin campaigned, Eleanor began to function as his conscience, advising him unofficially on what she considered to be ethical issues, although she always publicly denied taking this role. In any case, he did not always listen. Internationalists had rejoiced at Franklin's decision to throw his hat in the presidential ring in early 1932. So they were amazed when he announced early in February that membership in the League of Nations was a dead issue. Furthermore, he went so far as to suggest that cooperation among nations was no longer such a good idea for the United States, a position that Eleanor did not support. Pragmatically, FDR came to believe early in the 1932 campaign that it was no longer advisable to hitch his political wagon to membership in the League of Nations. By underplay- ing his former internationalist position, he hoped to defuse controversies that might torpedo his nomination and later his success at the polls.

Always a consummate politician, FDR sensed an isolation- ism welling up among Americans and veered away from con- fronting this trend. For several years he had tiptoed around the country's growing isolationism by keeping silent. Eleanor had been outspoken on this issue and on the ratification of the World Court, an international court of justice set up by the League of Nations to settle disputes between nations. Franklin apparently hoped he could slide by, letting her reputation speak for him with internationalists, without actually having to make a flat statement for or against. Growing numbers of isolationists feared these organizations as threats to national sovereignty and some even went so far as to accuse proponents of treason. FDR saw grave political dangers in these waters, and he didn't want to see the convention vote divided between the two factions.

So when newspaper publisher William Randolph Hearst demanded that Franklin take a stand, he quickly abandoned ship regarding the League of Nations. Had he been pressed, he was prepared to take the same position on the issue of mem- bership in the World Court. Eleanor was incensed that he didn't stand up for both the League of Nations and the World Court, and as Franklin told a friend after his announcement in the Hearst newspapers, "She hasn't spoken to me for three days."

No one knows, of course, what would have happened if Franklin had not satisfied the isolationists, but at the convention, when it came down to the final round of votes, it was William Randoph Hearst's influence that pushed Franklin over the top to win the nomination.

During the campaign that followed, however—because of his hesitancy on this and other controversial issues—Franklin had to fight a reputation for wavering and inconstancy of conviction, damningly described by journalist Walter Lippmann (in a column saved by Eleanor) as "an amiable man with many philanthropic impulses" who was "not the dangerous enemy of anything." Years later, Eleanor would admit to a friend that she would have voted for socialist opponent Norman Thomas in 1932, "if I had not been married to Franklin."

Franklin, meanwhile, valued her opinion, even when he didn't pay attention to it. The World Court was just one of many issues that she came to discuss with him during his political career.

In 1932, Roosevelt easily defeated Herbert Hoover for president, 472 electoral votes to 59 (with Hoover carrying only seven states). Eleanor was gratified at the victory she had helped fight for and pleased for Franklin, but at the prospect of life in the White House, she saw a pall drop over her own future. At 48, she knew her private life and much of the freedom she had enjoyed had come to an end. Her only hope, she recognized, would be to create a new life for herself within the context of the White House. "As I saw it," she wrote in her autobiography, "this meant the end of any personal life of my own. . . . I had watched Mrs. Theodore Roosevelt and had seen what it meant to be the wife of the president, and I cannot say that I was pleased with the prospect."

She had seen the dilemma coming. "Mrs. Roosevelt, aren't you *thrilled* at the idea of being in the White House?" one gushing reporter had asked the day FDR's nomination was announced in Chicago. She had puzzled some of the well-wishers gathered at the big house in Hyde Park when she gave only a solemn gaze in reply. One journalist, though, understood. Lorena Hickok of the Associated Press observed, "That woman's unhappy about something."

Lorena Hickok's perceptiveness that day soon formed a bond between the two women, and as the campaign extended from summer into fall, Eleanor began to take Lorena into her confidence. Despite what she saw in herself as rigidity, Eleanor had a passionate side, and she reached out to people who fulfilled her longing to be all-important to someone. She recognized that she would always share her husband's attention with his consuming political goals, and she would always share both him and her children with Sara Roosevelt. In any case, her children were all grown. Now she deeply needed to form bonds with people close to her, as she had with Earl Miller in Albany, and with Nancy Cook and Marion Dickerman at Val-Kill—people who responded with a special camaraderie, for whom she was a central figure in their lives, who would accept her affection, exchange confidences and let her help them.

And so, among those she thought of as close friends she now counted Lorena Hickok. They had first met in 1928, when Lorena was 35 and Eleanor was 44. Hickok had just joined the Associated Press in the flagship New York office as one of the first women reporters on the AP payroll anywhere in the country. The Democratic National Committee headquarters on Broadway was part of her beat, and Eleanor served as director of women's activities there during that election year.

Lorena was 5 feet 8 inches tall, weighed 185 pounds and telegraphed an accomplished, no-nonsense self-assurance. "Peering at whatever presented itself," wrote her biographer, Doris Faber, "her hands often clasped behind her back and her eyebrows slightly elevated as if some private joke were disposing her to a kinder assessment than might otherwise have struck her, she took the measure of any person or situation." When Lorena Hickok met Eleanor at the Democratic Committee offices, Hickok took note of that certain self-confidence that comes from being born into money; the clear, intelligent blue eyes; a pronounced overbite; and the stiffly self-conscious posture intended to hide her discomfort at being the tallest woman in almost any group. She also noticed a hairnet straggling unstylishly across Eleanor's high forehead, her unfashionably long skirt and unbecoming green blouse. Hickok was good at her job, and she landed an interview on November 7, 1928, the day after Franklin won the gubernatorial race. At the end of her article she wrote, "The new mistress of the Executive

Mansion in Albany is a very great lady." The comment was stricken, though, by her editor, who called it "too editorial."

Four years had passed with little contact between the two women, but when Lorena Hickok snared the assignment to cover Franklin's campaign train in 1932, she'd had an opportunity to get to know Eleanor better. By the first months of 1933, she'd been assigned to cover the wife of the president-elect, and her respect for Eleanor increased when Eleanor remarked in an impromptu speech at a party thrown by the Women's Trade Union League that she didn't intend to meddle in politics and then corrected herself, "I hope I shall be able to do a great deal for women. And when one does things for women, of course, one is also helping the men." Lorena Hickok admired this positive attitude and believed she saw the beginning of a campaign on behalf of women that she could heartily support. On February 15, Eleanor and Hick—as Eleanor called her—had enjoyed dinner together at an Armenian restaurant in New York, and Eleanor had dropped her friend off at the AP office on her way home. As Hick walked into the newsroom, the night editor shouted, "Where's Mrs. Roosevelt?"

A news release had just come over the wire that sent Hick speeding to 65th Street, where she found Eleanor looking pale as Louis Howe desperately tried to get a call through to Miami. A news flash had come through that the president-elect had been shot at while making a short impromptu speech in Miami, where he had moored his yacht during a fishing trip. That's all they knew.

Then another telephone rang. It was Franklin, calling to reassure Eleanor that he was fine and that she should go on with her schedule. Later, the details emerged: An irate brick-layer named Joseph Zangara had fired five shots from a cheap handgun, and one of the wildly aimed bullets struck Chicago Mayor Anton Cermak, who later died of his wounds. Under interrogation, Zangara insisted he had acted alone. "I want to make it clear," he declared, "that I do not hate Mr. Roosevelt personally. I hate all presidents, no matter from which country they come, and I hate all officials and everybody who is rich."

Afterward, Franklin insisted on accompanying Cermak to the hospital, holding the dying man in his arms. Finally, he returned calmly to his yacht when nothing else could be done. Eleanor and Franklin later talked over the dangers inherent in the presidency and came to the conclusion that since you could do nothing about that kind of danger, "The only possible course," she explained blandly, "is to put the thought of danger out of your mind and go ahead with your job as you feel you must, regardless of what might be called its occupational risks."

So now Eleanor calmly continued on with her planned trip, accompanied by Hick, to give a talk at Cornell University, attend an address by Pulitzer Prize–winning novelist Pearl Buck and attend a banquet that night. Soon they began planning a summer vacation together, motoring on the Gaspé Peninsula in Canada (something for Eleanor to look forward to after the inauguration), and Hick gave Eleanor a sapphire ring once given to her by an opera singer whose performance she had covered. Eleanor came to rely on Hick for decisions relating to her public identity and often sought her help when she needed a good editor's eye for something she had written. But most of all she relied on her for companionship, understanding and affection. When they were separated, they exchanged daily phone calls and letters—later, Eleanor wrote a sort of trial run of her column each day for Hick—and they spent time together whenever they could. Hick eventually resigned from the AP and went to work for Franklin's relief administrator and political consultant, Harry Hopkins. In those days Hick often lived in the White House, as did Harry and Franklin's secretary, Missy LeHand.

On March 7, Hick's 40th birthday, Eleanor wrote to her:

> Hick darling, All day I've thought of you & another birthday I *will* be with you . . . Oh! I want to put my arms around you, I ache to hold you close. Your ring is a great comfort. I look at it & think she does love me or I wouldn't be wearing it!

In the midst of her misery at becoming First Lady, Eleanor had found some solace. Initially, she had hoped that Franklin would ask her to be his official White House secretary, but when she broached the subject, his arched eyebrow and quizzical look gave her a clear message. Missy, he explained, would be upset. Eleanor once again had to forge a niche of her own—and develop her own ways of living in the glass bowl of the White House.

On March 4, 1933, when Franklin Roosevelt took office, the Great Depression had reached its lowest point. Using his now-famous line in his inaugural speech on the east portico of the Capitol that wintry day, he told the nation that "the only thing we have to fear is fear itself." He promised that if Congress failed to take broad measures to give relief to "a stricken nation," he would ask for "broad executive powers to wage a war against the emergency."

In an unprecedented 100 days of cooperation between the president and Congress, the federal government put an impressive series of measures into effect. Dubbed the "New Deal" by Franklin, the program included creation of the Federal Deposit Insurance Corporation and a series of federal programs intended to stimulate the economy and provide short-term jobs to get people back on their feet and believing in their country again. The New Deal programs were controversial then and still are now, and many economists argue that they did nothing to reverse the economic trends of the depression on the larger scale. But on the individual scale, they did make a difference in many people's lives. Eleanor was solidly behind the social programs of the New Deal, and she believed, as Franklin did, that the time had come when the morale of the people needed to be lifted, and that until this happened, no rise from economic depression would be possible.

With Molly Dewson, head of the Women's Division of the Democratic National Committee, Eleanor promoted the idea that women should be heard at every level of the new Democratic administration, and Franklin was all for it. He appointed Frances Perkins as his secretary of labor—the first woman chosen to serve in a presidential cabinet—and in this capacity she became one of the major architects and administrators of the New Deal's relief and reform programs. He also appointed Florence Allen as the first woman judge in the U.S. Court of Appeals. By the end of the first term, more women than ever before held government posts in Washington.

But Eleanor was quick to point out that Frances Perkins had worked with Franklin in New York State—as governor he had appointed her state industrial commissioner in 1929—and Eleanor insisted that she had little to do with these appoint-

Lorena Hickok, friend and confidante, with Eleanor on their trip to Puerto Rico and the Virgin Islands in 1934. (Franklin D. Roosevelt Library)

ments. But she did confess that she occasionally would "go to my husband to say that I was very weary of reminding him to remind the members of his Cabinet and his advisers that women were in existence, that they were a factor in the life of the nation and increasingly important politically. . . . As a result, I was sometimes asked for suggestions and would mention two or three names." For a woman who once had assumed politics should be left to men's superior capabilities, Eleanor Roosevelt had come a very long way.

In fact, she began to function as Franklin's "legs," traveling extensively on goodwill tours—about 40,000 miles during 1933 alone—winning friends for the New Deal, and at the same time inevitably inspiring criticism. Before long, she was saddled with the nickname "Eleanor Elsewhere." In 1934, Eleanor undertook a trip to Puerto Rico and the Virgin Islands. "I am going," she explained in her announcement of the trip, "because ever since the Puerto Rican Children's Feeding Fund was inaugurated by Theodore Roosevelt, I've been interested in the question of what really was the condition of people in Puerto Rico." She set off, accompanied by Lorena Hickok, at a grueling,

Eleanor with Malvina "Tommy" Thompson (left) and social secretary Edith Helm. (Franklin D. Roosevelt Library)

nonstop pace, to witness for herself what statistics had already told her of poverty and misery on the islands.

Because she saw and talked with a variety of people, Franklin came to depend on her as a sounding board, a reflection of people's thinking. "Often," she later recounted, "when some matter was being fought out with his advisers, he would bring up the question at dinner and bait me into giving an opinion by stating as his own a point of view with which he knew I would disagree. He would give me all the arguments that had been advanced to him and I would try vociferously and with heat to refute him." Then, his thinking solidified, he would often turn around and use Eleanor's arguments the next day in discussions with his staff.

On a trip to Appalachia in early 1933, Eleanor, and her good friends from Val-Kill, Marion Dickerman and Nancy Cook, paid a visit to a group of miners and their families in Morgantown, West Virginia. She and her friends were moved by their predicament, seeing the unsanitary conditions of the filthy, flimsy huts they lived in. Many of the miners had been blacklisted by the mine owners because of their organized labor activities, and Eleanor resolved she would find a way to help them.

Once back in Washington, she devised a plan for setting up a model for a large-scale homesteading program that Louis Howe was designing at the time. She convinced the government to purchase some land from a family named Arthur for this purpose, and the resulting undertaking became known as the Arthurdale Homestead Project. The plan called for construction of 50 prefabricated houses for the miners' families, at a federal cost of $2,000 each. Eleanor also set up a school there, based on the progressive principles she had learned while teaching at the Todhunter School. A factory for constructing post office furniture was planned to provide jobs.

Eleanor made many visits to Arthurdale, became personally involved with the miners and their families and learned a great deal about the hard life they lived. She encouraged them to preserve their folk traditions, and she offered compassion, sympathy and concern. But, though appreciative of her efforts, they were uncomfortable and suspicious of the government-run school and its fancy approach to schooling.

In fact, the whole project went badly. The houses didn't fit their foundations or the climate they were built for, and their construction ended up costing a whopping eight times the projected cost—about $16,000 per house. ("My missus, unlike most women," Franklin opined to his cronies, "doesn't know anything about money at all.") Critics both inside and outside the administration complained about the extravagance, and eventually the project was canceled. What Eleanor had hoped would become a kind of laboratory for social improvement at Arthurdale fell far short of her vision. But for the nation, the First Lady's identity as a reformer had been established.

Eleanor functioned in a way that few American women ever had—let alone a so-called First Lady—holding her own press conferences and commanding $1,000 per engagement on the lecture circuit. She was willing to speak, according to her speaker bureau's advertising brochure, on one of five advertised topics: "Relationship of the Individual to the Community," "Problems of Youth," "The Mail of a President's Wife," "Peace," or "A Typical Day at the White House."

During her years in Albany, Eleanor had been working on two major writing projects: *Hunting Big Game in the Eighties: Letters of Elliott Roosevelt, Sportsman*, which she edited as a tribute to her father, and *It's Up to the Women*, an anthology of articles that challenged women to become active in building a progressive nation. Both were published in 1933. She had also earned her own money with her radio appearances and writing. Now she came under fire for how she spent her money. She had helped the Women's Trade Union League by paying off the mortgage on their clubhouse and had used some of her money on the Val-Kill experiment. She set up lunchrooms for working women at the Women's Trade Union League clubhouse and the Girls' Service League headquarters on Madison Avenue. "I do not question that I often gave to people who were not worthy," she admitted, "but in those years it seemed better to take that risk than to fail those who were worthy." Later, she contributed to the American Friends Service Committee, who shared her philosophy that donations should help people help themselves. But critics contended that she was trying to evade taxes by having her income paid directly to the Friends. So she paid taxes and then donated. Throughout her husband's tenure in the White House, she found herself having to defend her financial affairs, but, in fact, she contended that she left the White House with considerably less than when she arrived.

Eleanor loved new beginnings. "There is something rather exciting about starting a new thing and one's ideas run riot!" she once remarked. So in December 1935, Eleanor began writing a syndicated newspaper column she called simply, "My Day." Fashioned on the idea that people would like to know what life is really like in the White House, she usually wrote a simple diary of her day, sprinkled with commentary and thoughts about issues and events that came up. It was homey and personable and, like her husband's "fireside chats" on the radio, made people feel like they knew the Roosevelts and that the White House was an extension of their home. It was a great success, syndicated in over 135 papers by 1940, and she continued writing it without pause (later trimmed down to three times a week after she reached her seventies). She missed a deadline only once, filing her stories even when she was traveling, and writing them out by hand when her secretary Tommy wasn't there.

As December sped past and Christmas came and went, the year 1936 approached, with another presidential election. By now, Eleanor was beginning to get used to life in the White House, but she still felt less than enthusiastic, writing to an old school friend, "I am quite overcome when I think of four years more of the life I have been leading!"

As the end of those first four years in the White House approached, Eleanor could look back on a period that had, as she had feared, left her with little time to herself. Yet she had found countless opportunities to be of service to the country, throwing her considerable energies into trying to relieve the widespread suffering caused by the depression. She had seen disappointments and setbacks, such as the Arthurdale Project, but she also completed the term feeling that overall she had made a real difference. For the first time the title "First Lady" had become more than just a social nod to the president's wife. Eleanor Roosevelt had begun to blaze a path that was uniquely her own.

7

REFORMER FOR HUMAN RIGHTS 1936–1945

A good many more than four years were in store for Eleanor in Washington, as it turned out. In June 1936, Franklin was nominated by acclamation by the Democratic National Convention. But Louis Howe was not there. He had died in his sleep in April. Eleanor felt she could sense a palpable loss in the wisdom of decisions made and feel the absence of the master engineer who always watched over his smoothly running machinery. She felt even as Louis fell ill that the mail wasn't analyzed well, and that Franklin no longer had access to as wide a range of people and opinions. Howe had always brought balance and steady-eyed analysis to the campaign trail. Now they would have to go on without him.

Soon after the convention, Eleanor prepared to work at the Democratic headquarters and then to accompany her husband on his campaign train. Initially, though, the Democrats thought it might be better if she kept out of sight aboard the train. The Republicans had begun to tout the fact that *their* candidate's wife planned to spend the campaign period at home, devoting her time "to the care of her family." (They knew, of course, that Eleanor wouldn't stay home.)

"Then it was discovered," wrote journalist Ruth Finney, "that the crowds wanted Mrs. Roosevelt. If she failed to appear on the platform they shouted for her until she did appear, and they cheered her just as heartily as her husband, sometimes more heartily."

Eleanor, in fact, had so transformed the role of the president's wife that at their annual party in March a group of newspaperwomen had put on a skit featuring a masked woman being interviewed to become First Lady. A delegation appeared to inform her that her husband had been nominated, but they explained, she would have to prove her own aptitude for the job:

"How many speeches can you make in twenty-four hours?" spoofed one.

"Have you ever gone down in a coal mine?" asked another.

"Can you write a newspaper column with one hand and shake 500 hands with the other?"

"How's your radio voice?"

"How many places can you be at the same time?"

"Can you remodel a White House kitchen?"

"How many states of mind are bounded by Reedsville, West Virginia?"

By this time, of course, the overcome prospective First Lady had fainted.

The campaign went well, despite Eleanor's fears, and Franklin won by a landslide, garnering 60.8 percent of the popular vote and securing 523 electoral votes, with his opponent, Alfred M. Landon of Kansas, winning only 8.

Before the election, in June 1935, Franklin had created the National Youth Administration (NYA) by executive order, in part in response to prodding from Eleanor. Now that the election was over, Eleanor turned her attention to this program for easing the plight of the nation's youth. "I have moments of real terror," she had remarked in May 1934, "when I think we might be losing this generation." Incomplete statistics from the 1930s show that some 30 percent of Americans between 16 and 24 who were in the labor market were unemployed.

A generation of forgotten youths was growing up in the nation's urban and rural regions alike, unskilled and untrained for productive work, lacking in self-esteem and ill-equipped in any way for the job of recovery that lay before them, and for which the nation depended on them. The establishment of the Civilian Conservation Corps (CCC) was the administration's first approach to the problem, sending thousands of young men into the woods to work on conservation projects. But this program had shortcomings. It was only for males, and it only helped those in dire need, who could do nothing else.

NYA, Eleanor hoped, would help meet the need for a wide-ranging program, based in home communities, that left the participants with new and reusable skills and, moreover, provided a program that included young women. The NYA incorporated and expanded on existing programs for helping needy college students stay in school, providing aid to transients and stimulating vocational training.

Though popular, the NYA was criticized both for undermining the self-reliance of all youngsters (if you give them a handout, they'll expect another, many critics claimed) and for including African-American youngsters. At a time when black Americans in many parts of the South—including Washington, D.C.—suffered the indignities and inequities of separate restrooms, separate seating on buses, separate schools, movie theaters and restaurants, many white Americans thought of African-Americans as second-class citizens. Eleanor Roosevelt had grown up surrounded by many of these same assumptions at a time when people—particularly in her social class—rarely questioned their own racial and religious biases. Now, for her, the severe economic pressures of the 1930s brought a different view to light. During the depression, the truth emerged that anyone could become destitute, no matter how self-reliant and independent and no matter what color the skin.

The more Eleanor probed at the racial issues she saw around her, the less she liked what she saw, and she became outspoken on the subject of civil rights. She went to visit black schools and communities, became friends with black leaders and saw the humiliation firsthand. Some of Franklin's advisers thought Eleanor went too far, spoke out too radically, and that she would rock the political boat that had swept them all into office. Some critics even began to accuse her of socialism, or even communism, but she still had many friends, and thousands of people continued to cheer her in the streets and at meetings.

But Franklin knew he couldn't stop her, even if he wanted to, and just as he had done with the World Court issue, he liked to let Eleanor put her foot in the water first to test the temperature. Then, with a little luck, he could gain credit for her liberal views among liberals, without losing the support of conservative Southern Democrats, an important part of his coalition.

Eleanor Roosevelt became an early beacon in the 1930s for the cause of racial justice. She began working with African-American educator Mary McLeod Bethune, who headed the Division of Negro Affairs for the NYA and was the highest ranking African-American in the federal government at that time. She and Eleanor became friends, and Mary Bethune often visited the White House.

But in 1939, when the two women walked into a meeting of the Southern Conference for Human Welfare in Birmingham, Alabama, they weren't allowed to sit together. Blacks and whites, they were advised, could not be seated together in a public gathering. Angry and stubborn, Eleanor refused to move. When she was told she was violating the law, she moved her chair to the neutral territory of the center aisle.

Just a few months later, Eleanor was again outraged when the Daughters of the American Revolution (DAR), of which she had always been a proud member, refused to let the accomplished opera singer Marian Anderson perform in their auditorium. Anderson, whom Eleanor had invited to sing at the White House in 1936 and who would later become the first African-American singer to perform at the Metropolitan Opera in New York, had a vast following, and the DAR's Constitution Hall was the only auditorium in Washington, D.C., large enough to accommodate those who wanted to see and hear her. Eleanor immediately resigned her membership in the DAR in protest, feeling that she could not remain affiliated with any organization that practiced such bigotry. Her action placed a spotlight on the ugly episode and created reverberations around the world.

The Department of the Interior came through, however, by arranging a free open-air concert on the steps of the Lincoln Memorial, where more than 75,000 people were able to hear Anderson's beautiful, clear contralto sing out. Significantly standing in front of the statue of the man who fought a war to abolish slavery for all African-Americans, and for every American, Marian Anderson sang "America," as she later said, "to the entire Nation." It was a triumph for racial equality and human rights for all—a triumph of the principles for which Eleanor Roosevelt had the courage to take a stand.

Eleanor continued to write during these years, setting down an autobiographical work, *This Is My Story*, which was serialized in the *Ladies' Home Journal* in 1936 and came out as a book in 1937.

In her personal life during these years, the biggest change came when she approached her friends Nancy Cook and Marion Dickerman about refurbishing the furniture factory as a cottage that she could use as a home base, with apartments for guests. For several years she had been subsidizing the failing business, and the suggestion no doubt seemed practical to her, but misunderstandings and hurt feelings ensued, and the breach never could be patched over. Nancy and Marion ended by moving out of all the buildings at Val-Kill and moving the furniture factory, vacating the premises for Eleanor. It was a sad end to what had once been a wonderfully supportive friendship.

Eleanor renovated the factory building, first fixing up a screened sleeping porch and apartment for Malvina

The living room of Val-Kill Cottage, 1956. (Franklin D. Roosevelt Library)

Thompson—Tommy—and then creating a cottage home for herself in 1937, with a cozy, informal sitting room focused around a fireplace, which became the hearth at which she would entertain many guests with charming casualness and hospitality for the rest of her life. In her kitchen at Val-Kill, she whipped up home-cooked meals that guests were expected to help out with and served them family style in her uncere-monious dining room. She called it Val-Kill Cottage, and it was hers. "My cottage," she wrote, "has a small apartment for the couple who work for me, two living rooms, a dining room, seven bedrooms, a dormitory for young people, two large porches downstairs and a sleeping porch upstairs. The cottage was an adjunct to our lives at Hyde Park but it was mine and I felt freer there than in the big house."

Meanwhile, trouble had been brewing in Europe, and by 1939, England and France had responded to aggressions by Germany with a declaration of war. Americans began to fear the ugliness they saw brewing there, and they eagerly sought to maintain continuity in their own country. Although no president had ever before run for a third term, if ever it sounded like a good idea the time was now.

Franklin was pressed into candidacy and concluded the 1940 campaign for his third presidential term by defeating his Republican opponent, Wendell L. Willkie, 449 electoral votes to 82.

Just seven months after his third inauguration, on Septem-ber 7, 1941, Sara Roosevelt died. By pure chance Franklin had gone to Hyde Park to see her the weekend of September 4. She had been ill at Campobello that summer but had seemed to recover, except for a slight cold. Franklin was stunned by her sudden death and deeply saddened.

On the night Sara died, Eleanor's brother Hall became gravely ill, following years of alcoholism and illness, and on September 25, after hospitalization for several weeks, he also died. The funeral was held at the White House, and Eleanor buried him at Tivoli.

"The loss of a brother is always a sad breaking of a family tie," Eleanor wrote, "but in the case of my brother it was like losing a child." The bond with her brother had always been close, and she had suffered to see him deteriorate, a victim of drinking binges and, as Eleanor put it, his own lack of self-control. "He had great energy, great physical strength, and great brilliance of mind but he never learned self-discipline," she wrote. For her own part, she felt both the sorrow of her loss and regret mixed with bitterness at the waste of what she considered to be her brother's great unfulfilled potential.

Two months later, the United States was finally drawn into World War II. On December 7, 1941, Japanese planes attacked the U.S. naval installation at Pearl Harbor in Hawaii, and, with no choice, Congress immediately declared war. Eleanor felt in this moment the deep anxiety and pain that any mother feels when her nation goes to war and she has children that she knows will be called to serve. All four of her living sons served during World War II.

At this point, Eleanor accepted the first and only "official" job she ever held in her husband's administration, the position of deputy director of the Office of Civilian Defense. She accepted no salary or paid expenses and worked long hours (occasionally going without sleep entirely). The mayor of New York, Fiorello LaGuardia, was director. Eleanor and LaGuardia differed in their views, however, with Eleanor placing more emphasis on morale and LaGuardia on preparedness. Unfortunately, too, controversies arose around Eleanor's appointment. Some newspapers claimed that she used the agency to employ her friends, and other critics again raised issues over finances. She later described the period as an "unfortunate episode," and LaGuardia finally resigned, soon followed by Eleanor.

"Never did I have more unfavorable press than at that time," she would later recall. Furthermore, she began to have disagreements with Franklin and members of his cabinet. Eleanor wanted to lay the groundwork for a broad-based health program that would continue after the war—not just for the military, but for children and young people as well. Harry Hopkins and Franklin were focused exclusively, though, on the exigencies of war. "I, however, could not help feeling that it was the New Deal's social objectives that had fostered the spirit that would make it possible for us to fight this war, and I believed it was vastly important to give people the feeling that in fighting the war we were still fighting for these same objectives." If Hitler won, all would be lost that they had fought

Newspaper cartoon (1940) depicting Eleanor Roosevelt's whirlwind travels.
(Franklin D. Roosevelt Library)

for so far. She fervently believed that the fight for the rights of minorities had to continue, even throughout the war years.

Once she had extricated herself from the Office of Civilian Defense, Eleanor was free to accept an invitation from the Red Cross to go to Great Britain as a goodwill ambassador, which she did in 1942. She followed that trip with tireless tours all over the world to visit soldiers, boost morale, see patients in hospitals, talk with children and dignitaries. Traveling through war-torn skies, the voyages were neither safe nor comfortable, but Eleanor never offered a complaint. In 1943, she visited American soldiers in the southwest Pacific, traveling over 23,000 miles in an unheated army Liberator Bomber. She lost over 30 pounds and almost exhausted herself before arriving safely back home.

At best, the press poked fun, publishing cartoons—the First Lady taking a whirlwind ride on a magic carpet; or a pair of miners who look up from digging coal to exclaim, "For gosh sakes, here comes Mrs. Roosevelt!" Typical of crank letters she received was one woman's accusation: "Instead of tearing around the country, I think you should stay at home and personally see that the White House is clean. I soiled my white gloves yesterday morning on the stair railing. It is disgraceful."

At worst, the press blamed her for her children's domestic foibles, an area in which she felt vulnerable and responsible herself. Ultimately, her five living children would have 19 marriages among them, with two ex-spouses committing suicide. "I don't seem to be able to shake the feeling of responsibility for Elliott and Anna," she wrote to Lorena Hickok during one difficult period. "I guess I was a pretty unwise teacher as to how to go about living." If she hadn't had so many outside interests, her detractors reasoned, her children might have had fewer problems. And if she couldn't teach her children, how could she claim to know what was good for America?

The years 1942 to 1943 were the strongest period of an "anti-Eleanor" backlash—even among some of Franklin's supporters who began to claim that her speeches, writing and influence were hurting Franklin. Opponents continued to accuse her of communist leanings, and the tone of the attacks became mean and personal.

When the election year of 1944 rolled around, Franklin was tired, but the war wasn't over. He had been a key player in negotiations among the Allies, meeting with Britain's Winston Churchill and the Soviet Union's Josef Stalin to forge policies for the postwar period they began to believe might soon arrive. Again, continuity was key, and so Franklin ran for an unprecedented fourth term, defeating Thomas E. Dewey 432 electoral votes to 99. Knowing that this would definitely be his last inauguration, Franklin urged Eleanor to invite all the children and grandchildren, resulting in a White House full of children of all ages. Franklin was in his element.

On February 4, 1945, Franklin attended the last of the wartime conferences of the leaders of the three powers. It took place at a resort called Yalta on the Black Sea in the Soviet Crimea. Churchill and Stalin met with him for the last time. They pledged "unity of purpose and of action." Franklin returned to the United States tired but gratified.

Two months later, on April 12, 1945, Franklin was at Warm Springs, Georgia, recuperating from a period of overwork, sitting for a portrait and preparing for a conference at San Francisco where the charter of the United Nations organization was to be drafted. Eleanor remained in Washington, as she often did, and on that day she attended a tea in her honor, a benefit for a charity of the Sulgrave Club in Washington. She was seated next to Mrs. Woodrow Wilson, listening as a concert pianist began her performance, when someone told her she had a phone call. It was Stephen Early, Franklin's press secretary, and he sounded upset. Would she come home at once?

"I did not even ask why. I knew that something dreadful had happened," she wrote later. She quickly expressed her regrets and left for the White House, hands clenched with anxiety. "In my heart I knew what had happened," she recalled, "but one does not actually formulate these terrible thoughts until they are spoken. I went to my sitting room and Steve Early and Dr. McIntire came to tell me the news."

Franklin had suffered a massive cerebral hemorrhage. Dr. Breunn at Warm Springs had done everything for him he could, but could not save her husband. Eleanor paused, then after a moment said, "I am more sorry for the people of this country and the world than I am for us." She summoned Vice President Harry S. Truman to inform him, then notified her children. Anna was nearby, but James, Franklin, Jr., and John were serving with the military in the Pacific, and Elliott was in England. To them she sent the message, "He did his job to the end as he would want you to do. Bless you and all our love, Mother." Quickly she boarded a plane to Georgia and flew through the night for a long, heartbreaking day at Warm Springs, the place that had always represented hope and vitality to Franklin.

Late that morning, the funeral train left Warm Springs for Washington. "The military guard surrounded the coffin in the back of the car where Franklin had sat so often," Eleanor wrote.

"I lay in my berth with the window shade up, looking out at the countryside he had loved and watching the faces of the people at stations, and even at the crossroads, who came to pay their last tribute all through the night." A funeral procession in Washington followed, white horses clanging their hooves on the pavement as they pulled the black caisson that carried Franklin Roosevelt's flag-draped coffin. The grinding of the iron rims of the caisson wheels could be heard above the muffled beat of drums, and hushed crowds lined the streets. In these broad streets, this same man had often flashed his winning grin and triumphant wave to cheering throngs. Finally, the caisson wheels turned up the gravel drive of the White House, and the coffin was carried up the steps as Eleanor followed behind.

Funeral services at the White House took place in the East Room, with the president's wheelchair sitting empty along the wall. Elliott had been able to return from England, and he and Anna both accompanied their mother, who was pale but composed. Then followed another long train ride, this time north to Manhattan and then up the Hudson River, through the grassy hills and budding trees of spring, to Hyde Park. There, in the military funeral tradition for a lost leader, a hooded black horse with a saber attached to its saddle and empty boots in the stirrups pulled the caisson home. The air rang with cannon salutes. After the burial service, Eleanor returned alone through a gap in the hedge and watched silently as workmen shoveled soil into her husband's grave. She was wearing a small pearl fleur-de-lis pin that Franklin had given her as a wedding present 40 years ago.

"I never realized the full scope of the devotion to him until after he died. . . ." she wrote. "Later, I couldn't go into a subway in New York or a cab without people stopping me to say they missed the way the president used to talk to them. They'd say 'He used to talk to me about my government.'"

Ever focused on building a positive outcome, in her column for April 16, 1945, she suggested, "that . . . a leader may chart the way, may point out the road to lasting peace, but that many leaders and many peoples must do the building."

Eleanor knew that Franklin had invited his cousins Laura Delano and Margaret Suckley to join him at Warm Springs, but she hadn't known that Lucy Mercer Rutherford was also there—the woman (since married) whose love letters Eleanor had found 27 years earlier in Franklin's luggage. It was Lucy who had brought the portrait painter, Elizabeth Shoumatoff. When Eleanor found out, and also found out that her daughter, Anna, had on occasion invited Lucy to the White House in Eleanor's absence, she was furious and deeply hurt. Not only had she not been with Franklin when he died, but the woman who had injured her most deeply in her lifetime had been present in a heartbreaking final deceit.

Yet, her son James told Eleanor's biographer Joseph Lash that his mother had never ceased truly caring for Franklin and that an "unshakable affection and tenderness existed between them." Eleanor had told her friends that she no longer loved him after her discovery of the Lucy Mercer affair in 1918, but that she stood by him only because she respected his leadership and believed in his goals. But Esther Lape told Lash many years later: "That is what she told me. That was her story. Maybe she even half believed it. But I didn't. I don't think she ever stopped loving someone she loved."

8

FIRST LADY OF THE WORLD
1945–1952

Now alone, Eleanor Roosevelt returned to Washington on the same train as the president, Harry S. Truman, and his wife, Bess. The time for changing the guard had arrived. The Trumans, as she later recounted, "were both more than kind in urging me to take my time about moving out of the White House, but I felt I wanted to leave it as soon as possible. I had already started to prepare directions so that the accumulation of twelve years could be quickly packed and shipped. As always happens in life, something was coming to an end and something new was beginning."

The process took her a week, and when she was finally finished, she held her last press conference, sat down to a last dinner in the family dining room and said good-bye to the view of the Washington Monument from her White House bedroom. The next morning, she had breakfast on the sunporch and she was off.

But Hyde Park was harder. Once James and Elliott had gone, and Eleanor settled in, she began to feel a huge void. (Hyde Park seemed all wrong without her family at the center, and Franklin at the center of that.) At least she had Fala, Franklin's dog, who now became a great solace, and she relished bathing him and putting him through his tricks, as Franklin had.

In May, Germany surrendered, and the fighting was partially over, with only the war in the Pacific area remaining.

A few days after Franklin's death, a reporter had approached Eleanor on the steps of the New York apartment she once had hoped Franklin would retire to. She looked at him and commented simply, "The story is over." And she believed it. She knew the rules of politics—when the reins are no longer in your hands, no one knows you exist, and that goes doubly for the wives of politicians. But this time—fortunately for the American people—Eleanor Roosevelt was wrong. The story was far from over.

Immediately suggestions began to pour in about ways people thought she could make contributions. She began to think about using her column to convert the nation's grief over the loss of a leader into an instrument for carrying out her husband's objectives. She became an interpreter and champion of his ideals. Initially, she planned to confine herself to radio and writing, and she turned down more than one request to do administrative work. But when George Carlin, head of the United Features Syndicate, suggested that she go to the Soviet

At the United Nations General Assembly with John Foster Dulles (left), George Marshall (on Eleanor's right) and Warren Austin, September 7, 1940. (Franklin D. Roosevelt Library)

Union as a correspondent—a trip she had longed to make—she was intrigued but decided to put it off.

Then President Truman, who had wanted to find an appointment for Eleanor in some phase of foreign relations, got an idea from Jimmy Byrnes, a man people used to call "FDR's assistant president." On the list of possible delegates for the first meeting of the United Nations Assembly in London, he told the president he would put Eleanor Roosevelt's name first. Because of her husband's interest in the success of the United Nations, he thought she just might accept. Immediately, Truman telephoned her, and she agreed on the spot.

During these postwar years, Eleanor began to lobby Truman about human rights, both domestic and international—and by now, she had broadened her scope and become more outspoken, no longer bound by being the wife of the president. It was not surprising when, as a delegate to the newly formed United Nations, she fought for the cause of human rights worldwide and became deeply involved in the formulation of the UN's position on human rights. In her capacity as UN delegate, she also championed the cause of peace and nuclear containment. She watched the Soviet delegates carefully and began to think, as she had learned about communists she had known in the United States, that their objectives frequently obscured the principles of honesty and trust. She grew to mistrust the Soviet UN delegates as well. Having visited a Nazi concentration camp after the war, she became a vocal advocate of the establishment of the uniquely Jewish nation of Israel.

In 1946, she became chair of the Commission on Human Rights, an auxiliary of the Economic and Social Council of the UN, spearheading the forging of the UN's Universal Declaration of Human Rights. In this capacity, she came to recognize the potential of developing nations, and she evolved an international world view that helped her immensely in her negotiations with other nations. She also realized that international relations could not take place without making allowances for diversities among the participating countries—especially with respect to economic conditions and cultural traditions. And she succeeded in steering the document through many hostile sessions. She tired of tedious Soviet attacks, "telling us what dogs we are," as she said, and the obstructionism she encountered. But she was patient and persistent and diplomatic.

In the end, at 3:00 A.M. on December 10, 1948, the Assembly, meeting in Paris, adopted the Universal Declaration of Human Rights. The final vote came to 48 countries in favor, none against, 2 absent and 8 abstentions (mostly members of the Soviet bloc). She had done it. In a rare tribute, the Assembly delegates stood to give a dramatic standing ovation to the woman who had made it possible.

The accolades rolled in. General George Marshall told the delegation that the 1948 session would go down in history as the "Human Rights Assembly." Charles Malik, who succeeded Eleanor as chairman of the commission commented, "I do not see how without her presence we could have accomplished what we actually did accomplish." John Foster Dulles sent a letter to the American Bar Association, of which he sent a copy to Eleanor. It was a defense of the Declaration:

> It is to be borne in mind that the Universal Declaration of Human Rights is not, at this stage, primarily a legal document. It is, like the French Declaration of the Rights of Man, a major element in the great ideological struggle that is now going on in the world, and in this respect Mrs. Roosevelt has made a distinctive contribution in defense of American ideals.

Eleanor Roosevelt deservedly considered this feat to be her finest achievement. And after its ratification, she devoted the rest of her life to the struggle for its acceptance in the United States and the world. Despite the long hours Eleanor spent on the Declaration of Human Rights and her continued travels, as always she kept in close touch with her family and friends.

In 1947, at the age of 63, Eleanor found another great friend, who also became a member of her select circle of friends. Fifteen years younger, David Gurewitsch was a doctor, a friend of her friend Trude Lash. David and Eleanor met on a flight to Geneva, and David soon became a frequent theater and dinner companion. She invited him to Val-Kill, where they enjoyed long walks together in the green Hudson River countryside. And when David married, Eleanor included his wife, Edna, in her circle. Ultimately, the three of them bought a town house in New York together, which they shared, dividing it up into two apartments. Eleanor had found a way to be less alone. The

Eleanor, November 1949, holding a poster of one of her proudest achieve-ments, the Universal Declaration of Human Rights. (Franklin D. Roosevelt Library)

Gurewitsches were delighted with her company and she relished theirs. Some friendships—with Marion Dickerman, Nancy Cook and Lorena Hickok, for example—faded away. But many she held close for a lifetime.

During these years, too, Eleanor's family seemed to gather around her. Elliott, who was divorced again, lived in Top Cottage at Val-Kill, a cottage that Franklin had built on a hill in anticipation of his retirement. Later, her son John and his family made their home in the little stone cottage that Nancy and Marion had lived in, while Eleanor maintained her homey living quarters at the refurbished furniture workshop, Val-Kill Cottage. Old colleagues from the days of the New Deal, friends both new and old, and visiting dignitaries alike felt at home there, where Eleanor's hospitality extended from flowers she picked herself for each guest to long-night reminiscences and debates.

Eager to help Elliott, who had ongoing financial problems, Eleanor formed a production company with him, agreeing to let him produce a television show for her. But Elliott continued to squander his money, selling off Roosevelt heirlooms and real estate to maintain his lifestyle and pay his debts. He sold the family vacation home at Campobello for $12,000. He sold a silver tea set from Eleanor's side of the family that dated back to Revolutionary War days. Then, without consulting Eleanor, he sold Top Cottage. For Eleanor, this was the worst betrayal, and she never really recovered from her anger with him, dissolving the company they had formed together. She had always been especially fond of Elliott, as she had of her brother Hall and her father. With all of them, she always felt a poignant sadness, even bitterness, about their missed opportunities and unborn dreams.

For her own part, the seven years following Franklin's death ranked among Eleanor's fullest, most productive and most independent. During this time, she had established firmly for herself a reputation as a clear, objective thinker, whose patience, political savvy and ability to look at all sides of an issue contributed to her effectiveness as a mediator and leader. She used these skills, combined with her keen commitment to fairness and justice for all, to focus an international light on the inalienable rights of human beings throughout the world.

9

ON THE WORLD CIRCUIT
1952–1962

Having completed her work with the UN Human Rights Commission in an exhausting all-night marathon session in June 1952, Eleanor hadn't planned to attend the Democratic National Convention in July, the first ever to be nationally televised. But she graciously accepted President Truman's insistence that she should come speak on the importance of the United Nations to the future of the United States. Her reception at the convention was a totally spontaneous and tumultuous roar of approval—described by the *New York Post* with the headline, "MRS. F.D.R. STOPS THE SHOW." The delegates finally quieted only after much gavel-banging by the temporary chairman, who pleaded, "Will the delegates please take their seats. Several million people are waiting to hear the First Lady of the World."

In her typical style, she accepted the welcome as a tribute to Franklin, not herself, and she incorporated her own memorial to him in her address, quoting from the Jefferson Day speech he had been working on at the time of his death: "If civilization is to survive, we must cultivate the science of human relationships—the ability of all people of all kinds, to live together and work together in the same world, at peace."

She made a mark, not only for the United Nations, but for the image of women in politics. "You really saved the day for political women. . . ." author and journalist Agnes Meyer wrote

Seventieth birthday at the Roosevelt Hotel in New York City. (Franklin D. Roosevelt Library)

to her afterward. "It certainly must have been a relief for the women of the country to realize that one could be a woman and a lady and yet be thoroughly political."

Eleanor had not endorsed any particular candidate, and she left the convention before the balloting began. Once the nomination settled on Illinois governor and former UN delegate Adlai Stevenson, she watched him with interest and was happy to offer him advice about his campaign, which he was equally happy to accept.

When Republican candidate Dwight D. Eisenhower was elected, however, he decided, in a clearly partisan gesture, not to reappoint Eleanor as delegate to the United Nations. He also accepted her resignation as the U.S. representative to the UN Human Rights Commission. But Eleanor had a deeply held commitment to the United Nations' work. She had even once remarked to a group of reporters that she wanted to spend the rest of her active life working for the UN. Now she made good on her word by volunteering to work for the American Association for the United Nations.

In the 1950s, Eleanor traveled widely—to Asia, the Middle East and the Soviet Union—continuing to wield her influence in the cause of human rights. She made two trips to Japan, visited Indonesia, Europe, South America, the Philippines, Thailand, Iran, Turkey and Morocco. Wherever she went, she met with women's groups, with students, with dignitaries and with children to talk about human rights.

Returning from one short trip in 1953, she came home to bad news: Tommy was in the hospital. Eleanor sped to her side. "For several days I spent most of the time there," Eleanor recounted. But when April 12 arrived, she visited Hyde Park to commemorate the anniversary of her husband's death. "On my return I walked into the hospital just as dear Tommy died. There had been no sudden change. She just died."

Malvina Thompson had been more than a secretary. She had been part of Eleanor's life for a quarter century, having joined her in 1928. "In many ways," wrote Eleanor, "she not only made my life easier but she gave me a reason for living. In almost anything I did, she was a help but she was also a stern critic. No one can ever take the place of such a person nor does one cease missing her . . ."

By 1956, Eleanor had warmed up to Adlai Stevenson, and she campaigned for his candidacy in two presidential elections—1956 and 1960. She was cautious about John F. Kennedy, however. She "would hesitate," she had said on national television in 1958, "to place the difficult decisions that the next president will have to make with someone who understands what courage is and admires it but has not quite the independence to have it." After the nomination, she was still uncertain she wanted to give him her support. But he was persistent, mature, charming and persuasive. Her sons James, Franklin and Elliott had all gone to work for Kennedy's election, and still she held out. Finally, though, he won her respect during a visit with Eleanor at Hyde Park.

In the course of their conversation, she began to see qualities she liked, after all. "When he came to see me at Hyde Park," she wrote in her autobiography, "I found him a brilliant man with a quick mind, anxious to learn, hospitable to new ideas, hardheaded in his approach. Here, I thought, with an upsurge of hope and confidence, is a man who wants to leave behind him a record not only of having helped his countrymen but of having helped humanity as well." A candidate, in short, that she could support with integrity.

Obviously conscious of her stature as a role model for young people everywhere, and especially for young women, she published profusely, including *This I Remember* (1949), *On My Own* (1958) and *You Learn by Living* (1960). During these years, she also collaborated with her longtime friend Lorena Hickok on *Ladies of Courage*, published in 1954. She continued to write her question and answer column for *McCall's*, which she had written monthly since 1949 (having done the same kind of column for the *Ladies' Home Journal* before that, during the years 1941–49).

In 1961, with John F. Kennedy in office, Eleanor once again became a delegate to the United Nations. Kennedy also appointed her as a member of the National Advisory Committee of the Peace Corps and chair of the President's Commission on the Status of Women. Kennedy, whose respect Eleanor had also won, encouraged her to write to him frequently to offer advice, and she did—about any issue she felt she could bring insight to, and he answered her gratefully.

Eleanor with President John F. Kennedy in March 1961. JFK was always grateful for her support during his campaign. (Franklin D. Roosevelt Library)

Now in her seventies, Eleanor appeared a bit old-fashioned for the 1960s, but she still had horizons to head for. "When you cease to make a contribution you begin to die," she wrote. "Therefore, I think it a necessity to be doing something which you feel is helpful in order to grow old gracefully and content-edly." True to her word, she became a visiting lecturer that year at Brandeis University and hosted a regular television show, called *Prospects of Mankind*.

She also still looked out for people in vulnerable positions. One day in New York City, a young African American acciden-tally backed his station wagon into her, knocking her down. She insisted she was fine, telling him to leave quickly before someone saw him, got excited and got him in trouble. She was bruised and scratched, but she continued meeting all her appointments that day without stopping.

On her 77th birthday she said, "I think I have a good deal of my Uncle Theodore in me, because I could not, at any age, be content to take my place in a corner by the fireside and simply look on. Life was meant to be lived. Curiosity must be kept alive. The fatal thing is the rejection. One must never, for whatever reason, turn his back on life."

By the beginning of 1962, Eleanor knew that she was winding down. As early as 1960, her good friend and doctor, David Gurewitsch, had recognized evidence that her body was not producing blood cells properly, a condition that would ultimately take her life. Though she tried to ignore her aches and pains, more and more Eleanor had to stop to sit down and rest, and she began to cancel appointments. She took time out to write some last requests. She wanted a plain wooden coffin, she wrote, covered with pine boughs from the woods she so loved near Val-Kill. That summer she entered the hospital in New York for tests and transfusions, which went poorly, and her recuperation was slow. Once released from the hospital, though, she mustered the energy to travel one more time to Campobello for the dedication of the Franklin Delano Roosevelt Memorial Bridge between the Canadian island and the United States mainland. On her way back to Hyde Park, she stopped to see her old friend, Esther Lape. "Then she went on to Val-Kill, where she had a few days and even worked," wrote longtime friend Trude Lash, who was with her. "But after Labor Day the fevers and the chills and the blood transfusions and endless injections took over and the lonely descent began."

Soon she was back in the hospital again, but from her bed she made her 78th birthday request—a birthday party with children. When October 11 arrived, a group of close friends with their children and grandchildren, gathered in Eleanor's New York apartment. There they celebrated with favors, ice cream, games and a birthday cake with just one candle glowing in the middle.

Back in the hospital, Eleanor began to refuse medication, clenching her jaws against pills and pulling out intravenous tubing. The end had come, and, unable now to function in the energetic way she always had, she had no desire to linger on in a hospital bed.

After suffering a massive stroke, Eleanor Roosevelt died November 7, 1962 at the age of 78 and was buried in the garden at Hyde Park.

As one reporter had commented after her last press conference prior to the 1960 presidential election: "She was a tall pillar of some quality no one else in our time has produced . . ." Her final work, *Tomorrow Is Now*, was published posthumously. It was a final statement of her belief that the ills of the world must be solved today.

EPILOGUE:

THE LEGACY OF ELEANOR ROOSEVELT

With her vitality, dedication and passion for reform, Eleanor Roosevelt produced a direct and telling impact on two generations of Americans—an impact felt at many levels and in many ways, for this was a woman of many facets. She was a leader of women's movements, a champion of African-American rights, a fighter for human rights worldwide and at home, a lecturer, a columnist and author. She served as unofficial American ambassador to developing countries and morale booster to American soldiers. She was a wife, mother and friend. She was a woman who fought for her independence, who overcame great sadness, grief and insecurities, and who forged a life of purpose out of the shreds of childish dreams and girlish hopes.

Today, her stature has become almost legendary. One sculptor, Penelope Jencks, struggling in the 1990s to capture the essence of Eleanor Roosevelt, dreamed that one day Mrs. Roosevelt walked into her studio, transformed in the sculptor's mind as a heroic figure 20 feet tall. This "20-foot" stature comes in part from what she represents for humankind—humankind's desire to do the right thing, her hard-won understanding and compassion despite her upper-class upbringing and background, her ability to look beyond herself and to probe broad issues of human equality and social justice. She provided a constant clarion call for justice, unflinching before the powerful

Eleanor, still tirelessly working in her late seventies, about to board a plane at LaGuardia Field. (Franklin D. Roosevelt Library)

in her determination to represent the rights of all human beings. Never so much concerned with ideology as she was with social justice, she was flexible and pragmatic, always looking for solutions that worked. And in her work with the United Nations, she showed an uncanny ability to understand and accommodate the exigencies of political reality.

Eleanor received no college education and no formal preparation for public service. Everything she learned—and her sum total of experience and wisdom became prodigious—she learned by experience and observation, by watching those around her, listening, reading and thinking. She learned early to think for herself and to judge for herself. No rubber stamp of her husband's administration, she fought for the kinds of human justice that appealed to her heart and soul—equality for African-Americans, a fair chance to earn a living for the average American, women's rights and the general well-being of the populace. She fought for these issues effectively and energetically.

But equally important as the issues she pursued is the way she pursued them—with an inquiring mind, eager to dig for the true facts and then act on them. "I think, at a child's birth," she once remarked, "if a mother could ask a fairy godmother to endow it with the most useful gift, that gift would be curiosity." It was her own finest asset. "I was not a gifted person," she once wrote, "but I was always deeply interested in every manifestation of life, good or bad." She continued:

> I never let slip an opportunity to increase my knowledge of people and conditions. Everything was grist to my mill: not only the things I saw but the people I met. Indeed, I could not express adequately the debt I owe to the friends who taught me so much about the world I live in. I had really only three assets: I was keenly interested, I accepted every challenge and every opportunity to learn more, and I had great energy and self-discipline.
>
> As a result, I have never had to look for interests to fill my life. If you are interested, things come to you, they seem to gravitate your way without your lifting a hand. One thing leads to another and another, and as you gain in knowledge and in experience new opportunities open up before you.

CHRONOLOGY

1884	Born in New York City, October 11
1892	Eleanor's mother, Anna Hall Roosevelt, dies
1894	Eleanor's father, Elliott Roosevelt, dies
1899–1902	Eleanor attends Allenswood School, a school for girls in England
1901	Travels to France, Italy with Mademoiselle Souvestre, headmistress of Allenswood School
1902	Leaves Allenswood after three years to make her debut into society
1903	Becomes engaged to Franklin Delano Roosevelt, a distant cousin
1903–04	Enrolls in Junior League of New York, teaching calisthenics and dancing to children in slum areas. Also helps investigate working conditions in garment factories and department stores
1905	Marries FDR in New York City on March 17
1906	Gives birth to Anna on May 3
1907	Gives birth to James on December 23

1909	Franklin, Jr., born on March 18, dies a few months later that same year
1910	Gives birth to Elliott on September 23
1911	Regarding the Women's Suffrage Movement, Eleanor states, "If my husband is a suffragist, I probably must be too."
1912	Eleanor attends her first Democratic Party convention
1914	Gives birth to the second Franklin, Jr., on August 17
1916	Gives birth to John on March 13
1918	Works with the Red Cross and the Navy Department to help American servicemen in World War II
1918	Eleanor discovers that FDR has had an affair with Lucy Mercer, her social secretary. FDR agrees to end affair. Eleanor and FDR decide against divorce, September
1920	Eleanor joins FDR in his unsuccessful campaign for vice president on the Cox ticket. Eleanor begins friendship with FDR political advisor Louis Howe
1920	Joins League of Women voters and works for women's political consciousness following the passage of women's suffrage
1921	FDR is stricken with polio. Eleanor nurses him and encourages him to work toward a return to public life
1922	Eleanor joins the Women's Trade Union League

1922	Joins the Women's Division of the Democratic State Committee and begins friendship with Democratic Party activists Marion Dickerman and Nancy Cook
1922	Eleanor actively joins FDR's campaign in support of Al Smith
1925	Eleanor and FDR build Val-Kill Cottage in Hyde Park, as a retreat for ER, Dickerman, and Cook
1925	Eleanor, Dickerman and Cook co-found the Val-Kill furniture factory
1926	ER, Dickerman and Cook purchase Todhunter School, a girl's school in New York City. ER teaches history and government there
1927	Eleanor becomes friends with Mary McLeod Bethune, president of Bethune-Cookman College. Through this friendship she gains understanding of the challenges facing African Americans
1928	Named the director of Bureau of Women's Activities of the Democratic National Committee
1933	Eleanor becomes the first First Lady to hold press conferences; only female reporters are admitted, March 6
1933	Eleanor helps to bring about Arthursdale, an experimental homestead project for West Virginia coal miners
1934	Helps initiate the National Youth Administration (NYA), which employed young Americans

1934	Eleanor works for antilynching legislation
1935	Starts publishing her syndicated column "My Day" in December, continuing until her death
1936	Eleanor helps Mary McLeod Bethune become director of the Division of Negro Affairs at the NYA
1939	Eleanor attends Southern Conference for Human Welfare meeting in Birmingham, Alabama with Bethune. Eleanor defies state authority by sitting in center aisle, between whites and blacks, after police tell her she is violating segregation laws by sitting with black people
1939	Helps to arrange a concert by Marion Anderson, a black singer, for 75,000 people at Lincoln Memorial
1941–42	Eleanor serves as assistant director of civilian defense
1943	Travels to South Pacific with Lorena Hickok to boost troop morale
1945	FDR dies. Eleanor comments, "The story is over," returning to private life at Val-Kill cottage in Hyde Park
1945	Eleanor becomes a member of the NAACP board of directors
1945	President Harry Truman asks Eleanor to serve as an U.S. delegate to the United Nations, and she accepts
1947	After being elected chairperson to the 18-nation UN Human Rights Commission, Eleanor Roosevelt be-

gins work on drafting the Declaration of Human Rights, January

1948	At the request of Truman, Roosevelt gives "The Struggles for the Rights of Man" speech at the Sorbonne during the General Assembly meeting in Paris
1948	Eleanor helps to secure passage of the Universal Declaration of Human Rights by the General Assembly, December 10
1950	Eleanor teams with her son Elliott and NBC on a television and radio show featuring famous guests, such as Albert Einstein and the Duke and Duchess of Windsor
1952	Supports Adlai Stevenson in his presidential bid against General Eisenhower
1952	Eleanor resigns from the United Nations delegation after the election of Republican president Eisenhower
1956	Taking a more active and central role in Stevenson's second unsuccessful bid for the presidency, Eleanor raises funds, unifies factions and delivers speeches during the campaign
1957	Travels to the Soviet Union for the *New York Post*, meets Nikita Khrushchev
1959	USSR leader Khrushchev visits Eleanor at Hyde Park
1960	Eleanor writes *You Learn by Living*, reflecting on experiences of her life

1960   Eleanor meets with John F. Kennedy, the Democratic presidential nominee whom she had opposed, at Val-Kill. She gains respect for him and begins to take an active role in the Kennedy campaign, August

1961   President Kennedy reappoints Eleanor to the UN and appoints her as the first chairperson of the President's Commission on the Status of Women

1962   Eleanor chairs an ad hoc Commission of Inquiry into the Administration of Justice in the Freedom Struggle; reports on the efforts and status of civil rights in America, Spring

1962   Eleanor dies in New York City on November 7 and is buried next to FDR at Hyde Park on November 10

FURTHER READING

Collier, Peter, with David Horowitz. *The Roosevelts: An American Saga*. New York: Simon & Schuster, 1994.

Cook, Blanche Wiesen. *Eleanor Roosevelt, Volume One: 1884–1933*. New York: Viking, 1992.

Faber, Doris. *The Life of Lorena Hickok: Eleanor Roosevelt's Friend*. New York: William Morrow and Company, 1980.

Freedman, Russell. *Eleanor Roosevelt: A Life of Discovery*. New York: Clarion Books, 1993.

Goodwin, Doris Kearns. *No Ordinary Time, Franklin and Eleanor Roosevelt: The Home Front in World War II*. New York: Simon & Schuster, 1994.

Graham, Otis L., Jr., and Meghan Robinson Wander, eds. *Franklin D. Roosevelt: His Life and Times: An Encyclopedic View*. Boston: G. K. Hall & Co., 1985.

Hareven, Tamara K. *Eleanor Roosevelt: An American Conscience*. Chicago: Quadrangle Books, 1968.

Kearney, James R. *Anna Eleanor Roosevelt: The Evolution of a Reformer*. New York: Houghton Mifflin Company, 1968.

Lash, Joseph P. *Eleanor: The Years Alone*. New York: W. W. Norton Company, Inc., 1972.

——. *Eleanor and Franklin*. New York: W. W. Norton Company, Inc., 1971.

——. *Love, Eleanor*. New York: Doubleday Inc., 1982.

——. *A World of Love*. New York: McGraw Hill Book Company, 1984.

Morgan, Ted. *F.D.R.: A Biography*. New York: Simon & Schuster, 1985.

Parks, Lilian Rogers, and Frances Spatz Leighton. *The Roosevelts: A Family In Turmoil*. Englewood Cliffs, N.J.: Prentice-Hall, 1981.

Roosevelt, Eleanor. *The Autobiography of Eleanor Roosevelt*. New York: Da Capo Press, 1992.

Roosevelt, Eleanor. *My Day: Her Acclaimed Columns, 1936–1945*. Edited by Rochelle Chadakoff. New York: Pharos Books, 1989.

Roosevelt, Eleanor. *My Day: Volume III: First Lady of the World: Her Acclaimed Columns, 1953–1962*. Edited by David Elmblidge. New York: Pharos Books, 1991.

Roosevelt, James, with Bill Libby. *My Parents: A Differing View*. Chicago: Playboy Press, 1976.

INDEX

Italic numbers indicate illustrations. The letter *c* following a page number refers to an entry in the chronology.